Well known to Australian and international viewers of Discovery Channel as the Aussie woman from the hit show *Gold Rush*, Tyler Mahoney is a fourth-generation gold prospector from outback Australia renowned for her drive and prospecting skills. After starring on two seasons of the spin-off *Gold Rush: Parker's Trail*, Tyler appeared on the flagship show in 2022 and is on a third season of *Parker's Trail* in 2023. Her success is a terrific example for any woman fighting to succeed in a man's world, and her struggles with bipolar disorder also make her a powerful advocate for mental health. Tyler has a podcast, *Let's Unpack That*, and a business, The Prospectors Club, dedicated to sharing her gold-hunting knowledge. *Gold Digger* is her first book.

TYLER MAHONEY

Published in the United States by Viva Editions, an imprint of Start Midnight, LLC, 221 River Street, Ninth Floor, Hoboken, New Jersey 07030.

Printed in the United States

Cover design: Steph Bishop-Hall © Affirm Press

Cover image: Beth Cunningham

Text design: Garamond Premier Pro

First Edition.

10 9 8 7 6 5 4 3 2 1

Trade paper ISBN: 978-1-63228-094-7

E-book ISBN: 978-1-63228-150-0

In memory of our Lucy. We remember you with every rainbow, every Taylor song, and every time we look up at the night sky.

AUTHOR'S NOTE

I wrote this book because I have always been told I am too loud, too bossy, too heavy, too thin, too intense, and too much. Throughout my entire life, people have tried to tell me what I can and can't say, what I can and can't do, what I can and can't be. Well, this is my chance to say that I can—and I did. I hope this book shows you that life is a lot better when you just be yourself.

This is a work of memoir; conversations and events have been reproduced to the best of my memory. I've also changed the names of some of the people mentioned to protect their privacy.

Most of this book was written in my home town of Kalgoorlie, on the lands of the Wongatha people. I would like to acknowledge that they are the Traditional Custodians of this Country and pay my respects to their Elders past and present.

And lastly, just a headsup that this book contains depictions of eating disorders, mental illness, self-harm, and suicidal behavior, so if these things are difficult for you, be kind to yourself and take breaks or skip sections if you need to. There's a list of resources at the back of this book if you need support.

CONTENTS

INTRODUCTION

The undeniable urge to hunt gold is programmed into my genes. I have tried to fight it, but the gold game has a way of pulling you straight back in. The best I can do to give outsiders an insight is this: imagine if your livelihood depended on the lotto or on a horse bet and then imagine the rush of dopamine when you finally win big. It's not surprising that many people dream of striking it rich in gold and go broke trying. As the saying goes—the best way to make a million dollars as a gold prospector is to start with two million. It's a hard game if you don't know what you are doing, and I am very aware of the massive advantages of being born into my family.

Growing up as a fourth-generation prospector, I had immediate access to experience and knowledge—equal parts educational, mind-blowing, and insane—that the vast majority of people will never get. A conversation with any outback gold prospector unearths stories and legends from a different world; the wild west may be the distant past for most people, but gold fever creates a culture of outlaws, gun shooting, gold stealing, outback rogues, and legends that persists in some of the country's most remote areas. Working with my family means that I've seen how gold fever impacts the beginners striking it rich, the experts going broke, and everyone in between.

Gold prospecting is the definition of unstable. Some days you will eat baked beans and others it will be lobster; you just pray you have more of the latter. The instability of the gold game is terrifying. I am paid a percentage of the gold we find every month, meaning if we don't find any gold, my paycheck is zero. It's an anxious way to live your life—not knowing if you can afford to feed your family, manage your car payments or, God forbid, survive unforeseen breakdowns and sickness. For me, the lure of striking it rich—the thought that tomorrow I could be a millionaire—outweighs any worries that this instability brings. I can not only detach from the anxieties but also place great faith in my ability to make it work. A life full of risk has always made me feel the safest and stability has always made me feel the most unstable. I still haven't figured out if this is due to being born into the wild world of gold, my bipolar diagnosis, my substantial fear of stagnation, or a mixture of all three—or whether this is toxic and delusional or endearing and brave, for that matter. Either way, you need to be partly crazy to make it in the gold game and I am yet to meet a gold prospector who doesn't fit that bill.

The magic of treasure hunting is exhilarating, but there are some pitfalls. Growing up in a world dominated by men taught me three things:

- I will always have to fight for respect.
- My looks will be judged before my abilities.
- Qualities that would be praised in men will be demonized in

women.

These lessons have shaped the person I have become. I have sat at many tables where I constantly had to earn respect while surrounded by my male peers who were handed it on a silver platter. It's taught me resilience and that, sometimes, being called a bitch is one of the biggest compliments a woman can receive. A bitch is a woman with boundaries, and I've been called a bitch for as long as I can remember.

All this knowledge has served me well in the complex world of gold hunting. It wasn't until recent years, though, that I realized this world, which at times seems mundane to me, is a world few people know anything about. It's a world shrouded in secrecy. I learned at a very young age to keep my mouth shut, but I believe these stories need to be told—especially those of my family. Our lineage of gold prospectors started over eighty years ago with Ned Turner, my great-grandfather. Ned was the pioneer for gold prospectors in our family. The famous Ned's Patch in the Murchison of Western Australia, where 800 ounces of gold was unearthed, with a value of over $2 million in today's market, is one of my family's greatest finds to date. We haven't given up.

It's in our blood.

1

THE OLD-TIMERS' GOLDEN
LEGACY

Ask any gold miner in the world and they'll tell you: gold fever is addictive. The glittering possibility of becoming an overnight millionaire grabs people and never lets them go. The chase for the next nugget is never over; there is always more gold to be found. The urge to just keep trying to make it big, and then bigger, drags you into an obsessive and endless cycle.

Gold fever has gripped my family for four generations. My ancestors first began their prospecting journey back when prospectors were pick-slinging men with beards, and loaming for gold—assessing gold content by hand-sifting through soil to determine how close you are to the source—was how you found the mother lode. Since then, we have spread across many parts of the Western Australian goldfields, from Norseman to Kanowna to Sandstone.

The Western Australian goldfields are exactly what you imagine when you think of the wild west. Their outback hues include bright reds, dusty oranges, and deep shades of rust all full of unimaginable history. My mum, Lecky, has always described our goldfields as brutally unforgiving, but endlessly giving. They are notoriously waterless, rugged, remote, and relentless. You need to be prepared and resilient when facing our outback because she will eat you up and spit you out if you drop the ball for a moment.

While I love my family's deep history embedded in the gold rush here, it is nothing compared to the 60,000-plus years of history and culture that the Traditional Owners have. The Wongi people have been thriving in the harsh conditions here for tens of thousands of years, and were the first people to find gold in the outback. They even showed Paddy Hannan—who later started the Kalgoorlie gold rush—his first nugget. Gold is important to the Wongi people and they worship it as part of their Tjukurrpa (Dreaming lore). If it wasn't for the Wongi people, I wouldn't be doing what I do now.

The First Nations people often helped the first prospectors: they showed them water sources and namma holes (like wells), local foods, where to find gold, and how to navigate. Many of the bush roads we use today were first formed in the original gold rush and often follow water sources. To this day, the First Nations people make some of the best prospectors in the goldfields; their knowledge of Country means they're very skilled at reading the ground and living off the land.

The gold world has created conflict ever since the beginning. The Traditional Owners' culture was displaced greatly by the colonization resulting from the gold rush. The prospectors disrupted the land immensely during their boundless digging for gold, and the introduction of alcohol, Western food, invasive species, and foreign disease wreaked havoc on the First Nations people in the area. The Wongi sporadically fought White colonizers who came to the area for gold in the 1890s. There was tension between the two groups and rightfully so—the European invasion was a time filled with death and loss, and its effects still make it difficult for present-day Wongi to thrive on Country.

It is important to keep in mind that my family's success in the world of gold comes from living and working on stolen land, which is not something to be proud of at all. My ancestors were among those who colonized Wongi, Yamagee, and Ngadju land, disrupting their culture forever. Although it's hard to think about my family's role in the displacement of Aboriginal people from their lands, it's important to talk about the history so we understand how we got to where we are today.

The gold story of the Mahoneys, my ancestors, started in the late 1800s when my grandfather's family traveled to Jimberlana, as it was known by the First Nations people, to try their luck prospecting. Jimberlana later became known as Norseman when local prospector Laurie Sinclair's horse, Hardy Norseman, kicked a large nugget out of the ground.

My great-great-grandfather was the first gold dealer in Jimberlana—well, first *illegal* gold dealer. He was also the local nightman, which meant it was his job to collect the thunderboxes every week. A thunderbox is what they called an outside toilet. I once asked my mum what they called the person who collected the thunderboxes and she replied, "Unlucky." It wasn't the most pleasant job. The nightman would stack the thunderboxes on a horse and cart and take them out of town to the desalination plant, where he'd rinse, restack, and then return them to the townsfolk.

Fortunately for my great-great-grandfather, collecting the thunderboxes gave him undetected access to the town's black-market gold scheme. His game was simple but thought out and, in an already lawless time, it was the recipe for gold-stealing success.

Local prospectors plagued with gold fever would steal gold from the mines they worked at; it was an unregulated, dog-eat-dog game. They then needed a way to sell this gold without drawing suspicion. So they would leave the lid on their thunderbox tilted to one side to alert dealers, like my great-great-grandfather, that there was gold sitting at the bottom.

My great-great-grandfather would stack these "special" thunderboxes separately and, once out of town, sift through the human waste to find the gold, weigh it, and replace it with cash. This ploy made him a better wage than gold prospecting ever could, and he was never caught. It's more proof that gold fever has turned people depraved since the beginning of time—if there is a will there is always a way. Over one hundred years later, my parents opened a store where they dealt gold (legally) for seven years—and the universe came full circle.

My ancestors eventually migrated from Jimberlana north to Kanowna, where they prospected for gold and opened Mahoney's Diner. Perhaps one of my favorite gold rush mining towns, Kanowna has a plethora of history and wild stories. At Mahoney's Diner, they would have served any food they could get their hands on—and only the well-off could have afforded to eat it. When you visit today, there's a sign designating where Mahoney's Diner once was, near some of the old infrastructure still lying where it collapsed a century ago.

Arriving at Kanowna today is a strange feeling. It's empty now—no buildings or trees in sight, barely any roads, and old miners' diggings scattered everywhere. You'd never believe that a little over one hundred years ago it bustled with more than 12,000 people and was full of pubs, hospitals, stores, and houses, or that a train from Kalgoorlie arrived every hour on the hour. Kanowna was the quintessential gold rush town, like something from an old Western movie: full of despair, loss, elated wins, secrecy, and gold fever.

It's fitting that my family has history in the old ghost town of Kanowna, because it's where my parents, my brother, and I prospect today. In 2010, over one hundred years after my family first came to the area, we acquired some of the original leases to ever be pegged in Kanowna, which I always find special. The Western Australian goldfields are vast, spanning over 770,000 square kilometers, yet our current mining tenements fall within kilometers of where my ancestors first set up shop.

Pegging a lease is the act of claiming new ground for gold prospecting; the process is archaic and hasn't developed much beyond what the original gold rush prospectors did. There's no technical land-buying system—you have to literally go into the bush at night when a lease is about to expire and hammer a peg into the ground at the lease coordinates. It's a bit eerie, waiting anxiously in the pitch-black bush and potentially racing others in the fight for sought-after gold-bearing ground. Of course, you can wait until daylight to peg your lease, but you'll most likely fall short: the lease becomes available at the turn of midnight, so the prospector's best bet is to fight for it then and there. It's a hard job; if the ground isn't surveyed, you need to hammer in four pegs to secure the lease, so the job is almost impossible alone.

In a place like Kalgoorlie, good ground is extremely hard to secure, so there will likely be a couple of crews trying to peg the same lease. It can get very heated—there might be fights, lies, and accusations—so we always make sure we film it. That way, if it goes to the warden's court, we have our proof. One slight mistake and you lose the lease, so you need to be on your game.

The Goldfields was a very dangerous region back when Kanowna was being established. The weather was intense: summer would see continual 104-degree days with no respite. Kalgoorlie's goldfields are known for their extreme lack of water and, unlike the Traditional Owners, colonizer prospectors didn't know how to find any. They had to travel hundreds of kilometers to find water sources in the grueling heat. If you visit any old gravesite hidden in the Western Australian bush you will notice that one of the most common causes of death cited on the headstones is dehydration; the other is disease. Prospectors were living in pop-up towns where unsanitary conditions, foul water, and overcrowding created the perfect conditions for a typhoid epidemic—the biggest Australia ever saw. Summers were long and hot, and help, resources, and medication were mostly out of reach. Striking it rich came at a great cost, but that didn't stop gold fever.

Around this time, in the early 1900s, new mining techniques flooded the goldfields from Kanowna to Coolgardie, Kunanalling, Sandstone, and everywhere in between. As a result, a slew of new safety issues followed—with no safety protocols in sight. Miners began to shaft deeper and deeper underground in pursuit of gold, sometimes hundreds of meters down. Shafts would often have offshoots that followed veins, the long ribbons of solid high-grade gold that form in rock, also known as the source or primary gold. Explosives were introduced, which meant miners could get deeper again. If heatstroke, dehydration, and typhoid weren't enough, these innovations now had miners succumbing to shaft collapses, rock falls, tumbles down shafts, and poor air circulation, among other mine safety deathtraps.

It blows my mind to find these shafts in the bush today and imagine heading down to work beneath their dodgy wooden collars. The rickety pillars in these shafts would support hundreds of tonnes of dirt while miners dug tunnels ten meters underground, so it's not surprising that so many men lost their lives. These tragedies paved the way for how we mine today—and it is like comparing apples and oranges. I'm sure the old-time prospectors would turn in their graves if they knew how much paperwork was involved for miners to even *think* about going underground.

We are often taught that it was the men who ruled the goldfields, who gave their everything in search of gold and risked their lives to find fortune, but women were really the backbone of the gold rush. They were the ones staying at home, raising the next generation, so their husbands could leave to find a mother lode. They were the ones at the forefront of nursing and hospitals, the ones widowed and raising families as single mothers, and the ones dying during childbirth at alarming rates on the goldfields.

Women weren't necessarily slinging the picks, but they helped make it possible. There is a way to go in leveling the playing field for women and men, and a good place to start is storytelling. My family has a long history of male gold prospectors, but in the early days it was their wives who made their careers possible. Not only did the women of the early gold rush manage the house and family, but they also left home to provide support onsite in the goldfields, saving lives and combating disease and illness.

The women in the goldfields weren't just holding the fort like my ancestors—they were also at the forefront of medical care, a very tough but essential job back in the day. The Coolgardie Museum tells the stories of Nurse Baseby, Nurse Penglase, and Sister O'Brien, three gold rush–era women I have always admired. In the early 1900s, they were among the first nurses to answer the miners' calls for help, leaving their families to care for the thousands of sick and injured men in the goldfields.

When Nurse Penglase heard how bad it was in the goldfields, her husband was working as a miner while she cared for their three children in Perth. She arranged care for the kids and set off to help. It must have been a hard call for a mother to leave her children, but she understood that people were dying and they needed her.

Nurse Baseby also traveled 600 kilometers from Perth to the goldfields in a bid to help those suffering in the harsh conditions. She set up the first tent hospital, which quickly became a maternity ward where she went on to deliver more than one thousand babies—mostly without a doctor. Many women and babies didn't survive childbirth in the goldfields, which made her job extremely emotionally taxing.

Sister O'Brien was also living in Perth when she heard about the squalor and disease rife in the goldfields. She was so horrified that she promptly left her husband and kids to help the miners through the typhoid epidemic. When Sister O'Brien arrived at Kalgoorlie, she went straight to the Exchange Hotel—still a busy venue to this day—and asked the warden to set up a hospital tent immediately. The warden granted her a plot of land next to the government hospital, which he also asked her to take over from the local constable, who was running it at the time. She agreed. According to records at the Coolgardie Goldfields Exhibition Museum, upon Sister O'Brien's arrival at the hospital, she described the patients to the warden as "the dirtiest looking objects imaginable, covered in dust and sand . . . the hopeless look of everything would have discouraged the stoutest heart."

A dire lack of water was among the greatest challenges nurses faced in the gold rush era. Prospectors today still struggle with water supply but it's incomparable to the old-timers' plight. These days, a 600-kilometer-long pipe supplies Kalgoorlie with water from the coast—something the early diggers could only have dreamed of. Water was rationed to extremes; there was simply not enough to sponge down patients struggling with fevers and heat. Instead of using water, the nurses would use whiskey—a liquid that happily never ran short in the goldfields.

These stories really strike a chord with me. These nurses paved the way for medical advancement in the goldfields, and it's heart-warming to reflect on the brave women who carried the gold rush. We give plenty of airtime to the stories of courageous men who risked their lives for gold and pioneered new mining techniques, but it's rarer that we celebrate the courageous women who got them there. It was their empathy and humanity that saved lives every day so the men could continue to work. The nurses who braved the harsh conditions to treat the sick were true heroes.

A progress committee, sent out to report on what was happening around the state in 1895, didn't have very much progress to report from Kanowna—but a telegram sent to Premier Sir John Forrest about the new town of Kalgoorlie warned: "Health of town most unsatisfactory. Fever spreading, deaths daily, and business threatened. No sanitary measures enforced or enforceable."

This message finally rang alarm bells, but it still took until 1905 to set up a Royal Commission to investigate ventilation and sanitation in mines across the state. Another followed in 1910, this time looking into pulmonary disease in the industry. By 1939, increasing mine safety measures—including up-to-code ventilation, certificates of competency, and protective devices (like boots and helmets)—was a government priority to try to curb the huge number of onsite injuries and deaths. According to the Department of Mining's report, in 1905 alone, 300 men were recorded dead or seriously injured due to mining methods—but this number probably falls very short of the truth. Mine managers were known to not record fatalities and injuries properly, and that figure doesn't even consider the men and women dying of disease, poor health, lack of water, and so on. After the Royal Commissions, mineshafts were fitted with structural support, sanitary conditions became controlled, sewage systems were implemented and, overall, all mining activities became more tightly regulated. These new rules transformed the goldfields from a lawless last frontier to a functioning industry more akin to the one we know today. After twenty or so wild years in the goldfields, the miners finally saw some relief.

Of course, any miner today will tell you that occupational health and safety has gone nuts—that you can't even sneeze without signing a piece of paper! We all like to whinge and moan about how safety laws have gone too far—I once couldn't enter a mine site because my shirt wasn't long-sleeved—but at least now we have a much better chance of getting home from work alive.

My great-grandfather Ned Turner was born in 1920 and entered the gold world after this industry-wide shift. Don't get me wrong— it was still the wild west, but the mining Royal Commissions had introduced a little regulation to the prospecting world by the time Ned entered it. He was one of the miners who lived through the single most notable advancement in prospecting history: the metal detector, which changed the prospecting game forever.

Before metal detectors, old-time prospectors had to find gold purely by reading the ground, loaming, and following the source. Back then, prospecting was heavily concentrated on hard rock, reefs, and lodes—depending on where you were in the Western Australian goldfields. Gold reefs, lodes, and veins are all names for primary gold, where the gold was formed. Gold generally forms in hard rock and thus needs to be extracted. Hard-rock gold is often found mixed in with quartz and ironstone, requiring retrieval via mineshafts, trenches, or costeans—a type of trench used to follow gold veins and to determine their size.

Alluvial and eluvial gold are secondary types. While alluvial gold moves away from the source due to water activity, eluvial gold is displaced from the source by erosion and weathering. Prospectors in goldfields with flowing rivers would pan the rivers for gold; in the desert, where my family is from, old-timers would use dry blowing and dry panning to retrieve fine particles—known as gold fines—and nuggets from areas rich in eluvial gold.

Today, the life of a prospector still pays homage to the old days. Just as we still peg leases on our goldfields, we still use a dry blower, the first-ever processing tool. Dry blowers came from prospectors needing to retrieve gold from paydirt without using water, and needing to adapt quickly. Ours is a lot bigger and more advanced than back in the day, but the fundamentals haven't changed.

Dry blowing started off as dry panning or winnowing, which was when the old-timers would use two pans to separate the "heavies" (gold and other heavier materials like black sands) from the "lights'"(sand and dirt). They would hold one pan that contained the paydirt in the air and tip it into another pan sitting on the ground, so that the wind would carry the lighter material away, leaving the heavies in the pan on the ground. This has evolved into what we do now: feed dirt with a loader into the hopper of our dry blower, which then pushes the dirt through the machine using air and vibrations. Gold is a lot heavier than dirt and naturally collects at the bottom of the riffles, which are bumps and dips in the tray for catching the gold. We collect that and then process it with a pan. The recovery rate is a lot lower than that of a wet plant, which uses water and is the preferred processing option when it comes to retrieving alluvial gold from paydirt, but you gotta do what you gotta do!

The Golden Mile in Kalgoorlie (the richest mile for gold in the world—and the reason Kalgoorlie exists) is home to 1500 tonnes of still-buried gold. Given that one tonne has a value of $70 million, it's easy to see why the gold rush is still going on today. The Golden Mile is also home to multiple types of gold, including alluvial nuggets, hard-rock primary gold, gold tellurides, and more; each type of gold requires different retrieval and prospecting techniques.

Take gold telluride, a rare metallic mineral. Due to its gold content, it actually has a silvery brass look similar to fool's gold. In the early days of gold mining, a prospector might be panning off some samples and notice a tail, which is when the contents of the pan fall to the bottom and clump together. A tail usually consists of gold and iron-rich material. If this tail was acting and moving like gold, but very dull in color, they would deduce that it was gold stuck in sulphides. When this happened, the prospector would burn off the sulphides on a knife blade over the fire. It's extremely dangerous to breathe in that kind of smoke, but that's what had to be done. As a little aside, in the early gold rush, gold tellurides were thrown in the waste piles used to pave the original streets of Kalgoorlie—so the saying "Kalgoorlie's streets are paved with gold" does have merit!

Prospectors found patches and the source gold by loaming for gold, a technique as old as the gold rush itself. Traditionally, loaming involved a prospector panning different samples from a spot, and if the sample produced gold, a white rock was placed to mark the spot. From there, the prospector would move left, right or up the hill in increments trying to follow the richer gold samples; source gold, generally sitting on a hill or rise, will emit traces of gold fines in the dirt below it, increasing in richness the closer to the source you get. If no gold was found, a black rock would be placed in the sample location and the prospector would move away. The prospector continues this method until they find the source, at which point a shaft will be dug and the prospector will pray they have found the mother lode. Alternatively, if the prospector found an ironstone or quartz reef (primary gold formed in a host rock of ironstone or quartz) they would follow the host rock until it ran empty. The host rock would then be removed and processed through rock crushers, or taken to the state battery to separate the gold ore.

Loaming really epitomizes what prospecting is all about: reading the ground, following the gold, and then knowing the best way to extract as much of it as possible. There is a huge difference between this and metal detecting. The old-timers could read the ground better than anyone and that is where they found their success—Sam Cash, the most famous loamer of all time, found over one hundred major gold mines in the Western Australian goldfields through loaming.

At the time my great-grandfather Ned got into the gold world, the proliferation of metal detectors gave prospectors the chance to find alluvial gold nuggets, which are generally scattered sporadically throughout certain areas. We often find a random nugget in the middle of nowhere with no gold around it, and these are the ones that weren't retrievable to the old-timers. We now loam with our detectors too—they bring a whole new efficiency to the game. As my family members always say, however, there is a big difference between a metal detectorist and a true prospector. You still need the skills to read the ground, to follow the gold. For us, mastering the techniques that the old-timers established is instrumental to being a successful prospector. It's a dying art that I never want to disappear.

Although Ned was there to witness the massive advancement of metal detectors, he didn't start out using them. Ned began his prospecting journey in a small town called Paynes Find in the 50s. Paynes Find is notorious for shallow ground, and is not known to have many alluvial nuggets. This isn't to say they aren't there, but the shallow ground paired with the town's proximity to Perth means it has been very well "smashed," as my father, Ted, would say; even the older, less advanced metal detectors can easily reach any gold there.

If you have visited any goldfields (specifically any goldfields where reefs, lodes, and hard-rock gold are prevalent) you will have noticed they are littered with mineshafts. A mineshaft is basically a hole in the ground where the miner has followed the gold. In the original Western Australian gold rush, shafting was one of the most common mining practices. The old-timers didn't have metal detectors to tell them where the gold was, so they had to follow it by hand and eye. Shafting was generally done to locate primary gold sources, and it was grueling, dangerous, exhausting work. Many miners did strike it rich but, as the saying goes, the people who were selling the shovels made more money than the ones digging for gold.

When Ned started his shaft, it was approaching the 1960s. Prospecting was much safer and more efficient than it had ever been: laws around gold mining had been established; towns had electricity and fresh water; sustainable nursing posts and hospitals were operating; residents had access to quality healthcare; mining equipment had advanced; and cars had arrived on the goldfields.

The work would have still been very intense, and I can imagine life was hard in the forever unforgiving conditions of the Western Australian goldfields. In 2019, I worked in Paynes Find prospecting a hard-rock mineshaft. It was essentially a modern version of what Ned would have worked on. I was there some sixty years after my great-grandfather, in the dead of summer. Even with air conditioning, fly spray, iceboxes, larders, running water, and all the other modern-day luxuries, it was some of the hardest work I've done. The flies were relentless. It may seem crazy to those who haven't experienced flies like that, but combine them with 100-plus degree heat, total lack of shade, and long workdays, and it was the closest I've been to going insane (and I've been close—more on that later).

The last point I will make about Ned is that he did find one of the Murchison's biggest known alluvial patches, just outside a town called Sandstone. Prospectors call areas that are rich in gold or areas where gold has collected in one spot "patches"; these range in size from football fields to several square meters. Patches aren't determined by area but by how much gold is found. If I found fifteen 1-gram nuggets in the space of 20 meters, I would say I'd found a little patch with a lot of small nuggets; if I found an area that stretched 1 kilometer long and 500 meters wide with 60 ounces worth of gold, I'd say I'd found a large patch with some good gold. Ned's Patch, which contained 800 ounces of gold, was roughly 500 by 500 meters and is still marked on local maps to this day. Today, that amount of gold has a value of $2 million, which is very hard to comprehend. Apparently, it was everywhere. They would walk around the patch picking up lumps of gold the size of tennis balls off the surface: a prospector's dream. Gold is getting harder to find, and an alluvial patch of that size these days is extremely rare.

My family has a rich history in Sandstone and today it's still one of my favorite places to be, even though it has a turbulent past. Sandstone became a ghost town after the end of the First World War when the miners were sent away to fight. This meant a lot of the mines closed, which had a domino effect on the town. Today, one hundred years later, it's still hanging on with a population of around seventy. There is no police station, no doctor, no fire station, and no hospital. If something goes wrong, you're in hot water.

I have a deep connection with the bush here and, without sounding too much like a crazy crystal lady, I truly do believe this is where my soul belongs. In hindsight (what a great thing) I have always been most balanced when I'm home in the red dirt; whenever I'm in our goldfields, my shoulders relax, my jaw loosens, my breathing slows, and my mind calms. A big part of this is because it's where 90 percent of my childhood memories have been made. It's all I've known. Although my comfort in the bush has a lot to do with the way it makes me feel, I also think there is something bigger at play, like my soul has existed here before.

Some people think of gold-prospecting as an old-timey hobby, a figment of colonial Australia. I can't blame them—my family's story is full of epic shootouts, injuries, thievery, kooky characters, and incredible finds both grand and grisly. Not to mention, the dramatic history of gold prospecting in Australia is well documented: heroic, mostly white men came from far and wide to try their luck in the goldfields. It was hard work, in a very romantic way: many suffered nobly, and some set up dynastic fortunes—or so we're told. As far as I'm concerned, at least part of this narrative is complete and utter bullshit. The truth is, we barely have a clue about the brutal and depraved realities beyond the glittery façade of our golden years. At the very least, I hope that sharing stories about my family and where we're from will highlight how the "official" history of gold-prospecting in Australia excludes nonwhite and nonmale figures, even though they were very much there and part of the action. A lot may have changed since (the distinct lack of typhoid is a plus) but gold fever never does. And for those of us under its influence, the stakes are higher than ever.

2

STAKING A GOLD CLAIM

As new and progressive social ideals swept across Australia in the 1970s, the goldfields braced for impact. Men had dominated the gold game since the beginning of the rush in the late 1800s, while women had always pioneered the medical, health, and safety fields—and of course, there were the amazing women who'd kept households afloat while their partners chased gold. But the 70s changed everything: women got behind the pick. Female prospectors were rare, sure—but they were there.

Two women in particular paved the way for me: my grandmother and mother. My grandmother was a third-generation prospector in the Mahoney line, passing the gold genes down to my father. Mum, on the other hand, didn't enter the gold world until later in life. Her dad was a car salesman and farmer, and she grew up in the Wheatbelt but traveled often with my beautiful grandparents, Ma and Pa, to remote areas of Western Australia. Mum fell in love with gold as quickly as she fell in love with Dad in the 90s. Once Mum got involved, she got Ma involved, who then began coming bush with us as well, which was very special.

My parents didn't start off as full-time gold prospectors living in the outback; they began as hobbyists. Heading bush on weekends and school holidays, I spent a huge chunk of my childhood in the desert watching them find gold. We would travel 700 kilometers over nine-plus hours to get to the good goldfields from our home in Mandurah, a city on the coast south of Perth. Dad had been immersed in the gold world since he was a young boy, but he worked at a manufacturing plant in Mandurah because they sorely needed the stable income, with two young kids and a mortgage to pay. We lived a fairly "normal" suburban sort of existence until death touched our family—and our lives changed forever.

Nola Ivy was my father's mother, and to me she was Na. Her death was the first time I experienced loss. I have felt it plenty since, but the day she left us was the day my heart broke for the first time. Na had been fighting cancer for eighteen long months; it was an excruciating battle and one we would realize was unwinnable.

Na knew her time was coming. My brother Reece and I were her only grandchildren, and we spent every Christmas with Na; she swore she would get one more with us. She held out for three months until Christmas morning in 2006, when she took her last breath. She was only 56. I find peace knowing that she had some control over when she would go—as much control as you can have when you're fighting the evil of cancer.

Our parents didn't tell us she had passed until Boxing Day. When I woke up that Christmas morning and asked Dad where she was, he said she was a bit tired and needed rest. I knew immediately inside my heart that she was gone. It was a strong feeling—like I could feel that her soul had passed onto the next phase.

I didn't say anything, though. I could tell Mum and Dad didn't want us to know yet. It still warms and breaks my heart that my dad said his last goodbye to his mother and then greeted us with a brave face when we woke, just to make sure we had a good day. My parents have always put our needs before theirs—no ifs, buts, or maybes. Dad would have been in so much pain, but he hid it all so he could carry it alone.

Na's funeral was the first time I ever saw my dad cry. Losing grandparents is extremely hard. I have never had to go through the turmoil of losing a parent, and I can't comprehend doing so while supporting the emotional and physical needs of two young children, like my mum and dad did. Grief is a weird thing. No one prepares you for it, and there are no rules. It's something we all must go into blindfolded.

I once asked Dad what he remembers most about Na: without a second thought he said her kindness. She was like a warm, buttery hug. As a child, she made me feel safe, heard, loved, and, above all, wanted. I never felt like a burden. Thanks to this unconditional love, this unwavering sense of absolute acceptance from Na and my family, little Tyler grew into the strong, confident, self-assured woman I am today. I never felt unwanted or neglected, and that is something I will be forever grateful for.

I think it's lovely that the first thing Dad says about his mum is that she was kind, because it's also one of the first words I would use to describe him. Dad always puts kindness before anything else: he is the first to help a stranger or give money to someone in need. It's a quality of his that I always try to emulate, and I guess I can thank Na for that.

Na was also one of the luckiest people I've met on and off the goldfield, and Dad always tells me that I have her luck—it's one of my favorite compliments from him. Na's lucky number seven is tattooed on my left hand.

Na grew up in Goomalling, a small farming town in the Western Australian Wheatbelt, and worked as the postie there. Dad always tells the story of how Na needed an ID for some paperwork, so— after twenty years of delivering the town's mail on a motorbike every day—she decided she'd better actually go and get her driver's license.

When she walked into the local cop shop to apply for it, the local cop goes: 'What do you mean, you've never had a driver's license? You've been the fucking town postie for twenty years!'

Baffled but enjoying a chuckle, he decided not to waste anyone's time with a driver's test. He handed Na her driver's license, and she went on her way. Only Na could drive around for twenty years and never need a license.

Na's prospecting journey looked a little different from the rest of the family's; she didn't get into prospecting until her later years but loved it with every bone in her body. Na was part of the generation that really saw technology proliferate in the prospecting world. Metal detectors were widespread, giving prospectors unprecedented access to alluvial and eluvial gold.

It was unfathomably exciting, and I would love to have prospected back then. If you speak to any prospector from that generation, they will tell you just how good it was and just how much harder it is now. It was around the 80s that metal detector technology created another gold rush, only second in size to the original, 100 years prior. A lot of older prospectors today will refer to those years as the good old days. Today, although we have soaring gold prices (gold would have been around $60 an ounce back then, compared to the astronomical $2500 an ounce now) and technology has advanced, nuggets are harder to find—the ground has been mostly picked apart.

I loved listening to Na's stories about the gold world. It always sounded so lawless, so thrilling. Back then, gold made the world go around. Towns like Kalgoorlie and its surroundings were built on gold—it was the reason everyone was there, and even today Kalgoorlie wouldn't exist without mining. If Kalgoorlie was the stage, gold fever brought the drama. One story from the 1950s in particular has always stuck with me—I still have a photo of the newspaper clipping.

It was 1952 when Victor Clark stole 36 kilograms of gold from the Kalgoorlie railway station—a month's supply of bullion that was in transit from Leonora to Perth when Clark intercepted it. Gold bullion is gold that has been melted down into bars, and is generally the end product of most mine sites. It is an investment and a worldwide currency. This gold was worth £14,000, or $2.5 million at today's price. Insane.

Clark was an employee of the railway line, which meant he knew the ins and outs of the system. Even though his inside knowledge set him off to a good start—especially since this was before security cameras—a colleague witnessed Clark steal the gold. The colleague later confessed in court that he kept his mouth shut because he didn't want to do his good friend in. That sort of loyalty was typical in those days—mateship was prized above all else. It's hard to imagine standing in court now and telling the judge you don't want to snitch on a mate.

In many ways, not much has changed on the goldfields. Na remembered that story from her childhood and now, some 70 years later, gold stealing is still rife. The judges are less forgiving these days and it's a little bit harder to pull off than just going to the storage room and taking a 36-kilo parcel of gold. Clark ended up fleeing on bicycle but was later caught by the gold police, which remains a very active division of Kalgoorlie detectives dedicated to gold theft. In 1907, the government was forced to set up the gold police to combat thefts just like Clark's: gold police tackling gold fever.

When Reece and I were kids, Na always joined us on our parents' long prospecting trips. She'd always loved the bush and the hunt, and by then she had split from my Pop, who wasn't in the gold world like she was.

On every trip, Na would make Reece and me these huge playboxes filled with paints, stickers, books, notepads, textas, and other arts and crafts to keep us occupied for hours on end. She always made sure we were happy.

I still remember one of the bigger nuggets Na found. She was always so expressive, so candidly elated. We still laugh about it today. We were at Barwidgee Station on the edge of Martu land, bordering the Western Desert. Everyone was going about their day when suddenly Na was jumping up and down, hands in the air, screaming: "Eureka! Eureka! Eureka! It's gold! Eureka! I've done it—it's gold!"

I was playing in a riverbed when I heard her and looked up to see her hopping about with glee. It's etched into my memory. Mum was 200 meters away and could still hear Na clear as day. She'd found a smooth 7-gram nugget that had traveled a fair distance in an alluvial wash. I still wear it on a necklace and think of that moment.

One thing my dad always says about gold prospecting is that if you love fishing, you'll love prospecting. It's the thrill of the hunt, and the patience required between the little dopamine hits. This was true of Na, who was also an avid crabber. I remember how she'd come back from crabbing sessions with buckets of blue manna crabs. She would then spend hours shelling them and making pickled crab—the best pickled crab ever, according to Dad. While I'll admit crabbing and prospecting have similarities, at least gold is worth a little more than a jar of pickled crab.

I am so thankful I got to experience the gold world with Na before she passed. I relate to her, and I feel we are very connected. Na experienced mental health struggles in her later years, which I had no idea about until she had passed. It's bizarre to think fifteen years after her passing that I am up against similar hurdles. I often wonder if my mental illness is hereditary or just unlucky. Hopefully, for my future children's sake, it's the latter.

When Na died, I was at the age where you are just starting to understand the permanence of death. Death has never been a taboo subject in my household; from as early as I can remember, Dad would say, "Everyone dies. I'll die. You'll die. Mum will die. There's nothing you can do about it—that's life. It comes, then it goes."

I still don't know if this outlook is morbid and warped or if it's just realistic, but I share it all the same. I'm not scared of dying at all. I know when it happens to me, it'll be time. It's part of why I find feeling stagnant so scary; I don't have long on this earth, and the thought of not achieving everything I want to before my time is up petrifies me more than death ever will.

In the early 2000s, both my parents lost their dads. Then when Na passed in 2006, it was the catalyst for my parents to drop everything, sell their whole life, and move themselves and us two young kids 600 kilometers away to chase gold full-time.

When I was ten and Reece was seven, they sat us down one day and said something along the lines of: "Kids, we know you love the bush and helping us look for gold. How would you feel about moving to Kalgoorlie so Mum and Dad can be full-time prospectors?"

Reece and I were both so excited—we thought it sounded like a great adventure! If any parent asked me this same question now, I'd tell them they're crazy. It was risky, leaving a stable job and income to move 600 kilometers away from any support to chase gold—especially with a young family. It was a wild leap of faith, and everyone else called them insane at the time, but this decision changed our lives forever. Not only did it put me in the middle of the gold world, but it also showed me that staying in your comfort zone is the surest way to kill potential.

My parents spent the next sixteen years working extremely hard, seven days a week every week of the year, to make that risk work. Their full-time gold prospecting job eventually saw them open the gold-dealing shop in Kalgoorlie, which they owned for seven years. It was hard work. They didn't take breaks and continued prospecting throughout those years, still very deep in the world—setting up mining operations, buying/owning/working leases, processing gold, and everything else that comes with the prospecting territory.

After owning the gold dealers for seven years and many, many successes, they realized true success to them was freedom, and it was time to pursue that. They sold the shop to go back to full-time prospecting, and today they're thriving. I think it's fair to say the risk paid off. I will always admire my parents for trusting their gut. They're the reason I will never let fear get in the way of my goals.

"Uncertainty," "risk," and "adventure" are three words Mum and Dad would use to describe raising two kids in the outback while they worked full-time as gold prospectors. Gold comes and goes—sometimes you're finding it, sometimes you're not. Kids are much more predictable—predictably needy and predictably expensive.

The pressure of managing bills, mortgages, food, sports, clothes, and the rest of it can outweigh the excitement of finding gold for prospecting parents—but, as mine always said, if you walk around the bush begging for gold, you won't find it. It's true: you always find gold when you're relaxed and enjoying yourself.

Dad first started going bush prospecting when he was a young boy and would frequent Sandstone with his grandfather Ned. By night, they'd sleep in swags on the grass behind the local pub, and by day they'd prospect. Forty years on, we often visit Sandstone to prospect as a family, and have even had a mining operation there.

To say Dad is a fount of knowledge on the area is an understatement. Dad is an extremely good bushman. It comes so naturally to him—not just the gold, but also navigating and reading the bush. It's like he was born 150 years ago in the original gold rush. He can visit a spot in the remote bush, find one good nugget, and locate the spot again ten years later at night without help or GPS. I've seen it time and time again.

Dad can look at a photo posted by another prospector of them standing next to a tree in the bush and, just by the type of tree and the look of the ground, know exactly where that photo was taken. I've seen him easily find tracks that haven't been used in fifteen years and are 400 kilometers from any type of civilization, just from a quick conversation with an old-timer two years earlier.

Meanwhile, Mum's disposition has always been her superpower when she's out prospecting. She might have only caught gold fever in adulthood but her calmness, patience, and meticulous technical skills meant she soon became highly respected in the gold world. She had to fight hard for that respect, though—it was still very much a boys' club. She showed me that I too could work in whatever industry I wanted, regardless of gender norms.

Together, Mum and Dad make such a dynamic prospecting team. Dad wanders the bush searching for new gold and ground, while Mum comes in and cleans it out like a human vacuum cleaner. Gold prospecting has never been about the money for them; it's always been about the lifestyle. They get to wake up in the morning and do something they love out bush, without anyone telling them what to do. This freedom is something I crave as well, and I will always be so grateful that my parents modeled it for me.

Both Mum and Dad went from not having a lot of money to running a multimillion-dollar business and successfully living as full-time prospectors—an epic feat to say the least. They have countless stories from their lives in the gold world, enough to write a book. Over the years, they've run a gold-dealing shop, started an open-pit gold mine, and tried their hand at heap leaching—a technique that uses cyanide to extract gold from ore—as well as managed scrape and detect operations, seen 100-ounce nuggets unearthed and beheld 1000-ounce patches.

They've seen the destructive side of gold fever more times than they care to—whether it's torn families apart, severed friendships or even claimed lives. My parents have traveled the outback and met a cast of quirky characters on the way—some of whom we call dear friends. They've seen prospectors find their fortunes, helped gold cops with busts, pegged leases, painted tenements, written mining proposals, and been through every inch of the Department of Mines's legal system. They've seen innovation, disaster, people at their lowest, and life-affirming acts of humanity. Thirty years in the game will do that.

✧

As prospectors, we always get the question: "What's your biggest nugget?"

I am sitting in last place with 5 ounces, Reece is sitting in third place at 7 ounces, Mum is at second with a beautiful 10-ouncer, and Dad is in the lead with an 11.5-ounce nugget. They aren't record-breaking numbers, but they do the job. Dad's 11.5-ounce nugget is a great story and so typical of him. He managed to find that whopper in an area that had been absolutely smashed. He is a walking gold magnet. Reece and I can work an area and find next to nothing but Dad will walk through an hour later, picking up pieces left, right, and center. Mum is similar except her gold skills come from patience; she lifts every stone and walks around every tree. You know that if Mum has done an area, it's been done thoroughly.

Personally, my favorite question to ask prospectors is "What's your coolest find?" You see their faces light up, and a lot of the time it won't be their biggest nugget. Mum and Dad's coolest finds reflect a lot about their personalities. For example, Mum is a collector, history buff, and a complete treasure hunter who loves a story. Her coolest find is up there with one of my favorites!

It was a hot spring day, almost summer, and Mum and Dad were out prospecting by themselves on a day trip. They were about forty minutes from town on ground that was flagged as pending, meaning it was in the process of changing ownership and was open for prospecting to the public for a short period of time. It was getting to the time of day when the joys of prospecting were quickly fading into "Fuck this, get me home." The flies were out in full force, the short mulga trees were useless in terms of shade, and the big ironstone ridges were a rolled ankle waiting to happen.

Mum decided to walk back to the car and, on the way, she kicked aside a big branch, swung her detector under it, and instantly heard the detector screech. Every prospector knows this type of screech—it was the type of sound we'd automatically assume was a bit of lead or a tin can, but could also be a very lucky day. She was tired and over it but, as all prospectors know, you dig everything. So one scrape of her foot and there it was: a golden sparkle.

As soon as you see that shimmer in the red desert, every irritation dissolves. The flies disappear, the temperature drops, and you are reminded why you love what you do. She bent down to pick it up and quickly realized it wasn't a nugget. Usually that would be disheartening, but not this time. Mum had yanked up a piece of gold rush history that a nugget couldn't compete with. As a treasure hunter, she was over the moon.

It was a man's 18-carat gold ring in pristine condition, which is shocking because it was date-stamped "1898." Next to the year, we could make out "Coolgardie Jewellers" in tiny script. Coolgardie Jewellers is a key part of Coolgardie history, a gold rush institution that is now long gone. When gold became scarce and Coolgardie quietened, many businesses moved on to Kalgoorlie. All that's left of Coolgardie Jewellers today is the jewelry.

The ring had sat there for all that time in the red desert, nestled in mulga scrub not a centimeter below the surface. There was no doubt it was a man's ring: it was very bulky and the size of my two index fingers together. What was interesting, though, was the four huge numbers protruding from the front of the ring: 3619. We knew they were there for a reason, but couldn't quite guess why.

The ring would have cost a fortune back in the gold rush days, when a lot of prospectors were just trying to find food to survive. They typically had enough booze and food for the week, a swag, a wheelbarrow, and, if they were lucky, a horse. Anyone spending money on things like jewelry back then was doing well—very well. We wondered if the ring maybe belonged to a warden, or a rich businessman passing through the area. It had to be someone with money to burn.

A couple of weeks passed before Dad figured it out: the four numbers were a lease number. Lease numbers look very different now; they have a letter and are five or six digits long, so that's why it threw us. But the old GMLs (gold mining leases, the richest original gold tenements) were only four digits long. We did some more research and there it was: GML 3619.

Suddenly, we had a story. So often we find relics and can only guess at the details, but not this time. We'd cracked the code and we were so excited. We suspected a prospector did extremely well for himself one day, pegged this GML, and then headed into town to celebrate. He probably spent money at the bar, drank the local Scotch, and may have visited ladies of the night. Clearly he had done *so* well that he had a huge, thick gold ring made featuring the four numbers that had made it possible.

That's our story anyway. Some 120 years after the ring was made, we ended up visiting that lease, which is now owned by a mining company. We told them the story and they thought it was spectacular. The poor bugger must have been spewing when he lost that ring somewhere in the desert, but it's safe with us now and something we will never part with.

Mum and Dad have found some brilliant patches in their time, but one they still talk about is the patch they found in eastern Murchison while on a ten-day prospecting trip with Reece. Virgin ground, the dream: untouched, no rubbish, and gold still lying on the surface left, right, and center, just like the old days.

This patch proves the one rule with gold that always rings true: there are no rules. For starters, it was exactly where it shouldn't be, and that's why no one else had found it. The ground was loamy with very short shrubs and hardly any mineralization. Not even the old-timers had found gold here back in the day.

My parents said they honestly found it by luck and normally would not have stopped for ground like that. Even though there are no hard and fast rules when it comes to gold, there are indicators that tend to point you in the right direction. This area was showing hardly any. Dad was just passing through, trying to get to some better-looking ground ahead, when he happened to hit a 40-grammer with his metal detector. He thought to himself, *What the fuck is this doing here?*

He decided to have a quick look around. Within half an hour he had a couple of ounces worth of nuggets, and he knew they were on. He went back to camp and showed Mum and Reece, who were as stoked as you'd expect. So they had some lunch and all three of them headed to the loamy, treeless patch to have a go. Three people detecting on the ground is better than one: you can cover much more ground, especially when you're on a time crunch and have to smash the patch before you leave. It was great to have Reece there; he is an extremely patient and thorough prospector. He does everything properly and is much more focused than me. My brain is so scattered compared to his.

There was only one problem: even though they were about 150 kilometers from the closest town, this loamy patch happened to be right on top of one of a mining company's main dirt tracks. It connected a satellite pit and the main camp, which of course meant it was the only busy track for miles and miles in any direction. The issue wasn't that my family were somewhere they weren't allowed to be—the ground was pending, so they had every right to be there—but that the area was massive. It was at least 1 kilometer by 500 meters, which is a lot of ground to cover with only a medium-sized, 19-inch coil metal detector. It meant they wouldn't be able to finish it all in the one trip.

They'd only packed enough food and water for a certain number of days (plus an emergency stash) and their rations were dwindling. So the plan was to smash out as much as possible, go home for a couple of days, and then return.

Another issue: if anyone was to see them at work, it would be game over. It takes just one person—one person from one of those cars driving past every day—to say, "Hey, there were three prospectors over at the flat. We should check it out." Word spreads like wildfire in the gold world, and if someone saw them in the patch, it was guaranteed to be completely smashed by the time they got back. Prospecting on someone else's patch is morally wrong and goes against all prospecting etiquette, but there are a lot of people who are desperate or greedy enough to do it. We call them gold poachers and they are just about as bad as they come. Although, in this case, if Mum and Dad weren't there working the patch, other prospectors might understandably have taken it as abandoned and finished it off themselves.

So Mum, Dad, and Reece spent the next three days diving and dodging at any sign of movement. I would pay good money to see my 100-kilogram, 6-foot-1 dad fully kitted up in detecting gear and jumping for cover behind shrubs every time a car drove past.

Mum describes it as a very stressful experience. They were on gold, but she knew it could be taken away at any second if a loudmouth spotted them from a car. Lucky for us, it was worth every single bruise on their knees (and probably ego) because that random, loamy, treeless patch was absolutely littered with gold. Those types of patches are what make gold prospecting worth it. In those three days the total weigh-up came in at 50 ounces—$125,000 for three days' work.

Afterward, they covered all their holes exceptionally well and ensured the area looked untouched before they headed back into Kalgoorlie. At the time, I was at home looking after the business and the house. They gave me a call and said they'd found 20 grams from the trip. I didn't say it out loud but I was thinking, *Well, fuck me, 20 grams isn't paying any bills.*

They were completely pulling my leg, of course. They wanted to see my reaction in person. They got home and we sat down at the table to do the weigh-up. Dad put 20 grams on the scales, and I said,

"Well, better than nothing." Then Reece slammed a 1-ounce nugget on top, and then a 2-ounce nugget, and then a handful of 15-gram nuggets, and another, and another. My jaw practically hit the floor.

Just when I thought they had stopped pulling this gold from under their seats, Dad chucked a 7-ounce nugget on top of the pile, tipping the scales to 50 ounces. I was gobsmacked. It's a very hard feeling to explain, seeing that much gold in front of you. After a couple of months of sweet fuck-all, we had finally hit a patch. We celebrated as a family and took a couple days off work before the three of them headed back north to finish the patch off.

They ended up finding another 30 ounces, meaning that area produced 80 ounces in a week's work. Patches that untouched are getting harder and harder to find, especially without getting machinery involved. Normally Mum and Dad would have considered pegging an SPL—a type of tenement that allows you the rights to prospect and mine using machinery—to get the machinery in once the leases went live, but the gold there was shallow enough to be found with a metal detector. If the gold was deep it would have been worth getting in a loader to scrape back the top layers of dirt to get to the source, but because they couldn't prove it at depth, there was no point. Still, it was a great patch and one they say they will remember forever. Mum and Dad have found some good patches before, but they loved this one because it was close to where they used to take Reece and me when we were younger. Mum said they had even driven past it before, so it was nice to do well in a place that had a lot of positive memories.

Every time I ask Mum and Dad about their fondest bush memories, their answers always revolve around us kids. This is so typical of my parents—everything they have done since the moment we were born was to help us, make us happy, or benefit us in the long run. They are two of the most selfless people I have ever met, and the love they have given Reece and me is unmatched.

3

BURIED OUTBACK SECRETS

Like my parents, most prospectors have many stories that they hold close to their hearts—but there are plenty of sinister tales out there too. The bush is beautiful, but it does hold a lot of secrets.

During the seven years my parents were the only gold buyers in Kalgoorlie, they became confidants to a lot of lonely people. My parents are trustworthy, and for many full-time prospectors, selling gold was the only interaction they had with the outside world. Prospectors would come into the shop and talk for hours, often telling Mum and Dad things they wouldn't tell anyone else. Prospecting is isolating; even though most of them love being alone in the bush, they still need that human interaction. For a lot of customers, Mum and Dad were counselors and a shoulder to cry on. My parents are such kind, beautiful souls, and it shows just how safe they made people feel.

Two stories from my parents' time behind the counter really stand out for them. One freezing-cold Tuesday morning in the middle of winter, the shop was dead quiet when Pete, one of Mum and Dad's regular full-time prospectors, came in to sell some gold. Mum served him, taking him into the back room to do the deal, but could tell something was off. He just did not seem like himself. Mum asked if everything was okay and he shared his story.

Pete had been prospecting on the weekend about half an hour out of town when he got a great signal, loud and shallow. He'd hoped for gold but, as he dug, discovered that the signal was alfoil from a packet of Benson & Hedges cigarettes. Disappointing, but a fairly standard occurrence . . . except that these cigarettes were still in someone's pocket, and that someone was still there, buried in a shallow grave. The grisly realization sank in: Pete had uncovered a human body—not just sitting under a tree but deliberately concealed in this far-flung patch of bush. He was horrified. He dropped the cigarettes and ran without looking back.

It shook him hard; in some Indigenous cultures that sort of discovery is associated with a lot of bad spirits and omens, and he wanted absolutely nothing to do with it. He never went back and never told the police, or any other soul, for that matter, except my mum—who kept the secret too. I have no idea how I would react to such a horrific find, but I know it would throw me. Mum and Dad often wonder who the man was, what happened to him, and where his body actually is, but they never asked questions. They just listened.

It's horrible, but it's not a total shock that there are bodies buried in the bush. This wasn't the first time a customer had confided something so troubling in Mum, but I think for her the hardest part to process was that the body's location was most likely intentional—that person was *buried* there. The prospector's information could have solved a missing-person case, or brought a family some long-overdue closure, but she couldn't get any more details from him. If she had gone to police, he would have just denied it and she would have tarnished her reputation in the community for being trustworthy.

The second time someone told her something like this, though, she did go to the police.

It was the middle of summer in 2008, and a man she had never met before came into the shop. His name was Shane. He was excited and curious about a cool treasure he had found in a remote part of Australia: a tiny vial on the South Australian side of the Northern Territory border.

Shane was a tour guide with no experience in prospecting, and had spent that morning at a caravan park in Kalgoorlie showing other caravaners the vial. One of them suspected it might be gold and suggested he come to see us to confirm. Shane hadn't even seen gold before, so that got him excited. One look at the vial and we confirmed it was indeed filled with gold fines. Shane was ecstatic. We got chatting and he told us very roughly where it came from, which sparked Mum's interest; she got Dad to come in and have a chat as well. This guy had found the gold vial sitting on a rock next to an old boot in a place not even close to a goldfield—like, I'm talking not even *remotely* close.

Straight away, Mum and Dad knew it was out of the ordinary. Had the man just come across a clue to an undiscovered goldfield? What was this vial of gold fines doing out there? Shane was over the moon; as a remote tour guide, a hidden gold adventure got him extremely excited. Mum and Dad were also intrigued because the vial could honestly have been 100 years old, maybe from an untapped gold source—it wasn't unbelievable.

The spot was hundreds and hundreds of kilometers away from any sort of civilization, and nowhere near any sort of phone reception, but Shane decided to head off on an adventure to find the hidden gold mine by himself. Back in 2008, people in the bush didn't have satellite phones and other fancy tech, so as a precaution he gave Mum and Dad a photo of the area so they would have a sense of the immediate surroundings if anything went wrong. He also told them roughly where he was going (very roughly, as he didn't want to give away the spot) and how long he would be gone for—information he'd also shared with one of his friends in Victoria. The plan was for my parents to contact the friend if Shane wasn't back in phone range by the arranged time. Mum and Dad agreed. They were more than happy to help and keen to see what he came back with.

A week before the agreed date came around, Shane walked into the shop. Mum greeted him with open arms, excited to hear all about the journey—except something was off, very off. Mum could tell right away that something had happened; Shane looked like he had seen a ghost, which wasn't far from the truth. When she asked what was wrong, he could barely get the words out. She sat him down and he explained that he had spent a couple of days relocating the rock and the old boot where he'd found the vial. It was still the middle of summer and extremely hot, so he was only exploring in the morning and afternoon.

He was taking samples, like Mum and Dad had told him to, when he came across something that would make the hairs on anyone's neck stand up. He found a small sandstone cave built into the side of a hill, very close to where he'd found the vial. He poked his head in and noticed a bend to the left. It was a very tight squeeze, but he crawled through to a point where the passage had been carefully sealed by old sticks and branches. Someone had purposely blocked off part of the cave with this barrier.

By now Shane was nervous, but still hoped he was about to clap eyes on the gold discovery of the year. He pushed back the branches, and his blood turned icy as he processed the morbid scene before him. He hadn't hit the jackpot; behind the carefully constructed stick barrier was the long-dead body of a man.

Shane let out a scream, scrambled backwards out of the cave, abandoned his search, and fled back into town. He told Mum it was a chilling experience, and Mum said she'd never been so worried for someone's safety after talking to them in the shop. He was so rattled he could barely talk about it, but it didn't take Mum too many questions to figure out this was a very old body; the old boot Shane described sounded like the type an old-time prospector would have worn. Shane wanted nothing to do with the gruesome discovery— he refused to see the police and wanted to pretend it never happened. Mum and Dad were the only people he told. After he left the shop that day, they never heard from him again.

It played on my parents' minds. Who was the person who died? What was their story? Dad has a theory that I think is spot-on: he believes a prospector was passing through the area when he succumbed to dehydration, crawling into the cave to escape the desert heat and die in peace. Dad thinks he had lost the plot by this point, because dehydration does that, and as a result he scattered his stuff—including the gold vial and boot—all over the place. *I* think he left them out as clues to any passers-by that he was there.

Either way, it still doesn't answer the key questions: did he find the gold there, or did he already have it? Why was he passing through such a remote area? If he was a prospector, he was a long way from any goldfields we know today—did he know something we didn't? All Mum and Dad had to go off was that old photo and a *very* rough 500-kilometer radius in the middle of Australia, so it would have been a fool's errand to attempt the mission.

Worried for Shane's wellbeing, my parents spoke to the local police about it this time. The cops said that there wasn't a lot they could do, going off a random photo and a guy's wild goose chase. They agreed the man was most likely a prospector who'd died of dehydration a very long time ago, and it should just be left at that. We still talk about this story to this day. We would love some closure, but out here that tends to be a luxury.

The best part of the gold prospecting is the freedom, and the worst part is the people. Gold fever is a real curse: it rips apart friendships and families, turns decent people into liars, and makes you wonder if there is anyone good left in the world.

Gold theft is a real issue in the goldfields and Kalgoorlie's gold police—the very same squad that foiled Victor Clark seventy years ago—never runs out of work. My parents became very well acquainted with the squad over their years in the gold shop. They'd help with all sorts of things, from identifying people selling stolen gold to assessing where certain specimens may have come from. But they never imagined they would personally require the gold police's help.

During my parents' time as commercial gold dealers, they stocked some of their gold nuggets at the Kalgoorlie visitor center for tourists to buy. As my parents started to get more sales, they stocked more and more gold there, until one afternoon they got a phone call from the gold police. It was gone—all of it. Someone had robbed the center overnight and stolen $30,000 worth of my parents' gold.

A woman who worked there—a woman who my parents knew— had given her work keys and the shop's security codes to her partner, who was a local drug dealer and user. He and another man raided the shop, stealing all our gold along with a lot of other valuable items. The woman and her partner then fled town, hoping to cross the state border before police worked out it was them. Happily, they were caught right on our border with South Australia. The man who assisted the raid was shot and killed in a dodgy deal gone wrong before he could be charged. My parents got the insurance payout but it's still a disheartening experience. There's no compensation for broken trust.

Being robbed by strangers is one thing, but being robbed by friends and family is a whole other ordeal. Mum and Dad have experienced this so often that their number-one rule is no partners; they work alone (except for my beautiful aunty and uncle, who are the only people they trust with gold).

There's never a nice way to be robbed, of course, but one particularly nasty incident changed their outlook on alliances in the goldfields forever. It was a Sunday, and Mum, Dad, Reece, and I all went out bush prospecting. Reece and I were still in school at the time, and Mum and Dad owned the gold shop but prospected on weekends.

Mum and Dad had killed the pig that day. They'd found a decent-sized patch in a section of a huge gold-producing area. They had worked with friends in that area for years, but this little section was known among the local full-timers for not having gold—which made their find all the sweeter. They were stoked to have found good gold in an area they knew others would avoid.

We had to head home that Sunday afternoon so us kids could get back to school and Mum and Dad could get to work during the week, but they were confident we'd come back the following weekend and the patch would be left untouched. We would normally never leave a patch unfinished, but we didn't have a choice.

Driving back into town, we spotted two of Mum and Dad's good mates driving along the fence line, so we pulled over and had a chat. The mates, Brett and Phil, were local prospectors who had held the monopoly in the area for a very long time. Mum and Dad had worked with Brett and Phil for years doing detect and scrape and other mining operations. The patch we found wasn't on their tenements—it was just on some mining company's pending ground.

Pending ground is ground that is pending tenement approval, a process that can take up to a year, and in the meantime the ground is available for prospecting by anyone using nonmechanical means. Prospecting on mining companies' pending ground is not an ethical issue at all and is completely legal, even encouraged. These mining companies aren't even interested in the alluvial gold that we find and they aren't going to miss the couple of ounces we normally go home with. Working a patch owned by a small-time prospector, however, goes against prospecting etiquette because you're taking all of their gold before they get a chance to mine it. Most prospectors understand the unspoken rule that if you are out in the bush and you come across prospectors legally working a patch, you turn around and mind your own business. If someone tells you they have found gold in an area, you forget you've heard it, especially if it's a mate. Prospecting someone else's patch is poaching and is "fucking low" as my dad would say.

Mum and Dad showed Brett and Phil the gold and told them where they had found it. The thing with my parents is their hearts are so kind; they would never think to raid another person's patch, and *definitely* not a friend's—and they expect the same respect.

The following weekend came, my parents returned to the patch, and there it was: the realization their "friends" were not friends at all. Brett and Phil had told other local prospectors every detail, and they'd come out to raid it, absolutely smashed it.

Mum and Dad were so disappointed that they wiped their hands clean after that; they left that area and never went back. It spoiled it for them—this place they had been working for years, with people they considered mates.

This sort of story is so common in the gold game. It wasn't the first or last time that "friends" leveraged my parents' kind hearts for their own greed—but not once has such an experience tainted Mum and Dad's morals.

Reece once suggested detecting a piece of ground that was being pegged by another prospector. Dad said there was no way and Reece responded with something like, "But he does it to everyone else!"

"I don't give a fuck," Dad replied. "We don't do that—we never have, and we never will."

And that's my parents to a tee.

✧

"I want to speak to the real boss—not you, the man."

It's a sentence my mum's heard time and time again working in this male-dominated industry. Mum has copped a lot of shit throughout her time in the gold shop and as a gold prospector. I've seen it my whole life, her being treated differently to my dad.

Watching Mum fight gender norms through her entire career really inspired me to do the same. She once told me, "I worked so hard to prove my worth—to prove that I was a good gold prospector. I worked so hard, and after years and years they finally started to see how good I was. Ounces and ounces of gold later, I finally did it: I earned the respect I deserved." I asked if Dad had to fight for that same respect. Her reply: "Oh, no, he was handed it." And that's the issue.

Mum was never taken seriously in the gold game, but instead of letting it get to her, she made it her strength. Men would openly tell her their secrets while trying to big-note themselves: "Oh yeah, I found a four-ounce nugget over that hill!" one would say, or "Last week I got fifty-five grams over on Donkey Flat." Prospectors who were typically tight-lipped were more than happy to share their secrets with Mum because they thought she posed no threat.

Mum would just nod and smile, listening carefully and taking advantage of their small-minded assumptions by making note of the information they gave her to build her mental picture of gold-producing areas. There weren't really a lot of women doing it when Mum started out, especially no full-time prospectors. She didn't meet another until 2018—they were extremely few and far between. It was always her and the blokes. She held her own and showed me that I too could be a prospector.

One time Mum, Dad, and a friend were on a prospecting trip north, all sitting around the campfire after a day of detecting. Their friend, Martin, made a comment about a laterite breakaway a couple of hills east. Mum went to say that she had noticed it as well and had seen the old chop holes on it—which means that a prospector had been there digging up signals they had found with their detector, presumably gold in this case.

Before she could get the words out, Martin interrupted her.

"Oh, Ted, I was talking to you. Lecky, I don't think you would have made it that far," he said.

Mum quickly shut down that ridiculous comment. "You mean the breakaway with the chop holes all over it?" she replied. "Just because I'm a woman doesn't mean my legs don't work as well as yours. I actually found a three-gram nugget just past it, it's a shame you didn't find anything!"

Dad instantly had her back with a giggle: "Mate, she covered more ground than you did today."

This is the norm, especially in gold: the immediate assumption that women are less capable, less fit, less intelligent, less skillful, less talented than their male counterparts. It may not seem like a lot to men—you know, sticks and stones—but these words have power. They can erode confidence and inhibit women from backing themselves in the already-tough gold world. It's hard enough believing in yourself without all the men around assuming you're inadequate.

The men of the gold world eventually realized how good Mum was—so much so that she once had an ounce hit on her back: one of our prospector friends said that if anyone could find gold in a spot after Mum had done a sweep, he'd give them an ounce of gold. No one has ever been able to claim that ounce.

One positive of all of this is she has always had Dad standing by her side, unwavering in his support. It's sad that his support is necessary; Mum is more than capable of handling herself. Still, I feel blessed to have parents with such strong respect for and connection with each other—and I'm especially grateful that they both taught me to back myself and recognize prejudice at play, as it was on that night around the campfire.

4

GOING FOR GOLD AND
BUSH FIXES

Guns, gold, graveyards, and generators—growing up out bush was one hell of an experience.

All my earliest memories are set in the remote desert of Western Australia: wandering the land, racing motorbikes, setting off fireworks, exploring old mines, wrangling cattle, and trying our best to find the mother lode.

Every weekend and school holiday, my brother and I would fend for ourselves in the desert while my parents searched for gold. Well, "fend for ourselves" is probably a little dramatic; we were fed and looked after, but a lot of our time we had to make our own fun. When we were lucky, we would also have our younger cousins or station friends join us on our adventures.

I remember being in primary school and all my friends talking about the cool trips their family would be taking on the holidays.

I also remember thinking to myself how lucky those kids were, because once again the Mahoneys were just going out bush. Now I realize I truly took that for granted. I have the best childhood memories, memories that are rare, and I would never change them for the world. I wish eleven-year-old Tyler understood this a little more.

In my early childhood, when we lived in Mandurah, Dad worked full-time and Mum took care of the home but they both still prospected when they could. We would travel more than nine hours to get to decent gold areas every school holiday and long weekend and were always tight on money—but my parents never burdened Reece and me with that stress. That's another thing I have always admired about my parents: they carried their own issues privately and let us kids be kids—although they managed to ensure we weren't completely sheltered either. For as far back as I can remember, they instilled resilience in us. When I have kids one day, I want to replicate this aspect of their parenting. They struck a good balance between exposing us to the real world and sheltering us from adult issues. They never let money, or lack thereof, curb our happiness as a family unit. When we lost Na so young, the grief only spurred Mum and Dad to make the most of the time we have together; it was part of the incentive to move to Kalgoorlie.

It was a big risk, but loss made my parents realize the importance of not being a "Gonna." They always said that there is no better way to waste your life than constantly saying "I'm gonna": "I'm gonna start a business next year"; "I'm gonna move to Italy when I feel ready"; "I'm gonna write that book when I have more experience."

People who always say "I'm gonna . . ." are the ones who always stay in their comfort zone, and I've learned that nothing truly amazing or life-changing happens there. "Don't be a Gonna," Mum and Dad would say, and these four words have stuck in my mind for life.

When people ask me how I started my businesses or achieved any other milestones, I always tell them that "Don't be a Gonna" was ingrained in my brain. It's there every time I decide; it's there every time I tell people I am going to do something. I think it's another reason I get anxious when I'm *not* acting on a new idea I have. My brain works in extremes, but in moderation this mindset is a huge advantage. It means I action most of my ideas and desires, so I'm not a Gonna. I've also learned to do so after critical thinking—something I'm still working on, but that I'm grateful I was taught as a child.

These are the best memories I have: the childhood years following my parents through the bush with a pick any spare second I had. At the time, though, I didn't always see it like this. I was always so embarrassed to tell people I was a gold prospector. I thought people would judge me because it was weird. A huge majority of the kids had parents working on the big gold mines, but little-league gold prospectors like my family members are rarer.

Kids tend to harshly judge anything that deviates from the norm. I also thought I would be judged because gold prospectors were stereotypically old men living in the bush, and I didn't want the other kids thinking my family was like that. This crippling shame continued into my early adult years, and it's funny to reflect on now because gold prospecting is my *thing*—and it's led to a lot of my success. Being a gold prospector, I am somewhat unique. The one thing about myself I tried to hide for so long is the same thing that has brought me the most blessings. Its clichéd, but being different is a strength. It's what makes us memorable.

At school it was a little running joke to call me the Gold Digger, a term clearly rooted in sexism. While it was all fun and games— and there are *much* worse things to be called—it still brought me shame. Tall poppy syndrome has a lot to answer for in Australian playgrounds. Things have a funny way of going full circle, though: now I get to celebrate that title, Gold Digger, which used to bring me shame, as the title of my first book. I wish I could go back and tell my fifteen-year-old self to own my uniqueness.

Another quality that set me apart at school: I was never a demure, delicate sort of girl. I was the type of opinionated, independent girl we like to refer to as "bossy"—another insidious term designed to bring down women. I also wish I could tell fifteen-year-old Tyler to embrace the leadership qualities that were demonised as "bossy." I mean, how dare a young girl use her initiative to plan or problem-solve?

Just as kids need to be guided on the "rules" of our world— things like manners, kindness, and work ethic—they need help navigating their own innate, unique qualities. I wish adults would tell the bossy girl in school that her proactive approach and influence over her peers might make her a great team leader one day, whether that team's a squad, a business, or a country.

One of my favorite stations we visited when I was a child is Banjawarn

Station, a huge cattle station that lies on Kuwarra land. It's a wild place about 400 kilometers north of Kalgoorlie and it covers more than one million acres.

The first time we drove there to go prospecting, it was 2006. We were in our little old Datsun ute, the old Dado—Dad's favorite. It was aqua green, had no air conditioning, and would shut down every time we drove through a puddle. As we pulled into the station, the wires in the car ignited, causing a small fire. Dad didn't show it, but I can imagine it would have been stressful, being stuck 300 kilometers from the closest town with your wife, two young kids, and no car. Not ideal.

Luck was on our side that day; it turned out the station owner had the exact same car sitting in their wrecking yard. We grabbed the wires out of that, and it was as good as new. This was also the first day we met our station friends, Chelsea and Ben. I spent a lot of my childhood on this station and some of the neighboring ones hanging out with Chelsea and Ben, so we became very close.

The first time we met them, Reece walked up to Ben and introduced himself. Ben, who would have been eight, headbutted Reece right in the nose and made it bleed. Still not *quite* sure why he did that, but it was a good start to the friendship. Naturally Chelsea and I, the two older sisters, formed an alliance too. It was a love–hate relationship between the two teams, sisters versus brothers, constantly at war.

Chelsea and I would set up our base camp in the orchard, while the boys claimed a junk pile of old cars, machinery, and parts 200 meters away. The orchard was cool, shielded from the sun, and scattered with old trinkets. It was a haven for native birds and bees, filled with citrus trees, passionfruit vines, and, my personal favorite, the mulberry trees. It was like our little oasis in the middle of the desert. We spent hours climbing the mulberry trees and their fruit became a staple in our diets. We'd feast on the berries until our faces were covered in bright red juice, and then spend just as long trying to remove the stains with green mulberries afterward.

One day, Chelsea sent me to the top of the mulberry tree to pick some fruit. One of us would pick the berries, place them on a leaf, and drop them down for the other to collect. As you can imagine, gravity stopped this from working as efficiently in real life as it did in our heads—so we tried to come up with other mechanisms to get the berries to the ground. On this day, we created a mulberry-carrier-bucket attached to a rope so we could place the berries inside and slowly lower them down. Suffice to say, we thought we were the next Patricia Bath.

As I climbed up the tree to install our million-dollar idea, my foot got stuck in the nook of two branches. I tried to jump free but got stuck even more awkwardly, falling straight out of the tree and landing smack-bang on my left arm. I let out a scream and Chelsea came running. The pain was excruciating, but I couldn't tell our parents because I was too embarrassed.

As a child, I always felt embarrassed by pain and vulnerability. I am not exactly sure why, but I think there are a few reasons. I remember as a young girl I once tripped and badly scraped my knee out bush, and a family friend said, "You're brave. Don't cry—brave kids don't cry." It just stuck with me. I have always wanted to be seen as brave, and not annoying or getting in anyone's way.

I grew up in the gold world where everyone was rigid and hard, especially the men. I was never exposed to much vulnerability. Men didn't cry where I was from, and I didn't want to burden anyone with my tears. I grew up seeing injury as a weakness—and this mindset has never left. Even today, it causes havoc as I try to manage my mental health.

Having since snapped a fibula while surfing, I am almost certain that when I fell out of that tree I fractured my wrist. Of course, I wouldn't let Chelsea tell anyone I was hurt, so to fix the sore arm we wrapped some mulberry leaves around my wrist—I am not quite sure what the logic was behind that—and continued our berry-picking operation.

The pain got worse over the following days, during which us kids went down to the sheepyards to help with shearing. This was back when stations in this part of Australia could have sheep; these days, they are few and far between due to the wild dog problem that has escalated a lot over the past fifty years, especially since the government stopped culling them. When I couldn't join in with the other kids, the adults became suspicious. I ended up telling my parents, who were a little confused as to why I hadn't just said something—which didn't help my case when I tried to explain how painful it was and that I was certain it was broken.

We were a nine-hour round trip from the closest hospital at this point, so a dash to emergency would have cut the prospecting trip short, and we really needed gold as we hadn't hit our target yet. So, like many things that break in the outback, my wrist got a bush fix: Dad cut out some cardboard from a cereal box and used that as a splint with some bandages. It hurt for the next couple of weeks but that was the end of that.

I knew from a young age that gold was important, and if we weren't finding it, we went without. This was another reason I felt shame around pain and vulnerability; bad decisions that Reece and I made impacted our family financially, and I hated putting that stress on my parents. I would rather stay quiet and in pain. My parents would be horrified to learn I did that, but it's just how I reacted as a young child.

On another visit, Chelsea and Ben took me into their "classroom," which was an old *donga*—a portable structure common in the outback. Most station kids do School of the Air, which Chelsea and Ben did until middle school. Station parents help, or they have a jackaroo/jillaroo to help with the schooling. Jackaroos and jillaroos are usually young people working on stations to learn the ropes. They help with everything that it takes to run a remote station and really do need to be a jack/jill of all trades. Living in such a remote location can mean you're cut off from the rest of the world—when we were out on Banjawarn Station, we didn't have a computer, let alone the internet. Chelsea and Ben hadn't even heard of *The Simpsons* when I first met them.

School of the Air is a real blessing for remote kids—it means they can stay with their families on the station and still receive a decent education. Often these kids help out with work on the station and fit in schooling when they can. It's a completely different lifestyle from that of a "normal" student, but I thought it was great. You do go without a lot of things, but staying onsite means you get to experience some amazing moments that very few people are lucky enough to experience in their lifetimes.

On one trip late into the year, we went to a neighboring station called Yandal, which Chelsea and Ben's dad did the caretaking for. It was sweltering hot, up around 120 degrees Fahrenheit, and there was no air conditioning. The "lounge room" was one of the only places to escape the heat—barely. It was just an outside area with a roof, surrounded by four dongas. All the rivers were bone dry, the dams were stagnant, and we were 800 kilometers from the ocean, so our favorite way to cool down was to take cold showers every fifteen minutes (not that desert water is ever actually *that* cold) and lie in the shade as we dried.

The days consisted of a lot of trough runs to make sure the cattle had water, and we aimed to avoid the sun completely between 10 a.m. and 4 p.m. I've always been a big daydreamer; on days like that I would lie there for hours fantasizing about a cold Coke from Macca's and a swim at the local pool. At that time of year, we would often see bungarras (a type of massive lizard) that lived under the dongas. They were everywhere and us kids would get into trouble for leaving food out for them.

The donga out the back was where my Na and her pet kangaroo, Missy, would stay. We found Missy in her mother's pouch, barely alive after being hit by a car. I would walk up to Na's donga with Reece at night to hold Missy, and we would argue over who was going to do the last feed before dark.

We would spend hours in the creek—or rather the swathe of cracked dirt that we called the creek—behind the main shack, digging for water to make mud pies. We would often get four feet deep before we reached it, and then head back for lunch at the main shack, which was two adjacent dongas connected by a veranda.

Under the veranda was a living area with an old fireplace, and I have a very faint memory of a fifty-cent coin being superglued to its concrete floor. I looked when we went back years later, and it was still there. As kids, we would think it was truly hilarious every time an adult bent down to pick it up.

Life as a station kid, hey.

Dreaming up new business ventures was very common for me as a child—I have nature and nurture to thank for my entrepreneurial streak. Independence has always come naturally to me: I am a big believer in astrology—I think my deep need and desire to be my own boss is half- due to my heavy Sagittarius and Capricorn placements— but I also think a few key life experiences and role models nurtured the businesswoman inside me.

I remember one such experience from when I was in Year 5. I asked the teacher what an entrepreneur was, and she responded, "Oh, it's an old white man." I'm guessing she didn't realize they would burn into that little girl's brain forever when she said those words to ten-year-old me, but here we are all these years later and it's still something I think about regularly. It was at that point I thought, albeit in a more Year 5 sort of way, *What the hell? If they can be one of those, then I can too.*

This is the earliest memory I have of questioning gendered power imbalances and deciding to make it my life's mission to prove a point. Proving a point has been a prominent theme when it comes to my life decisions, and I'm not too proud to admit some points would have been best left unproven.

I also have my parents to thank for my enterprising spirit. We originally moved to Kalgoorlie so they could prospect full-time but, shrewdly identifying a gap in the market, they opened their store soon after our arrival.

Kalgoorlie, the gold capital of Western Australia, didn't have a gold buyer until my parents set up shop; before then, any prospector wanting money in exchange for gold needed to travel 600 kilometers to Perth to cash it in—very inconvenient for a normal person, let alone for a prospector. The trip to Perth to sell the gold would often cost more than the gold itself, and they needed that money to survive, so my parents were busy from the get-go and enjoyed great success.

I started helping Mum and Dad in the gold shop when I turned thirteen. Working so closely with my family was pure joy and made this job one of the best gigs I ever had—although it did ignite in me a strong resentment for working for most other people.

I learned that working with gold meant coming face to face with gold fever. Lies, theft, and more lies were par for the course. It became hard for me to trust people. Working in Mum and Dad's gold shop, I started to realize the true scale of the gold world's underbelly—and just how quiet my voice was in a room full of men.

5

BUSH LESSONS AND STRANGE NEIGHBORS

It's funny how when you grow up out bush, you learn things that just become second nature. On stations and when camping, most of our power comes from generators. We'd always turn off our generators around 7 p.m. once dinner and showers were all sorted, so we got used to living in the dark without TV or computers to entertain us. Once the generators were shut off, it would be time for bed so we'd be ready to get up at the crack of dawn the next day.

We were taught to always carry a torch and wear shoes when walking between dongas, houses, tents, or toilets at night—but of course, when you're a kid, you think you know more than your parents. One night I was walking between dongas with my station friend, Tim, when—*hssssss*—he stepped, bare-footed, straight onto a king brown snake. We recognized it instantly as one of the most venomous reptiles in the outback and dashed for the safety of the nearest donga. Miraculously, he wasn't bitten. I always wore shoes at night after that. (And then always checked them in the morning before putting them back on, just in case a deadly spider had crawled inside!)

The more I faced the consequences of ignoring my parents' advice, the more it sank in just how dangerous the bush can be. Of course, as a preteen you still think you are invincible, so I learned a lot of bush lessons the hard way—from motorbike accidents to getting lost in the wilderness.

Working in the male-dominated gold world, I also soon learned that my voice didn't count for as much as those of my male peers. It gave me a huge insight into the danger of associating with the dodgier side of that world too. When things went awry, the consequences were serious and sudden, and I realized that navigating it all as a young woman meant I had to be extra vigilant.

It's strange to feel so at home and safe in the bush, yet still always slightly paranoid about what dangers might be lurking just out of sight. Take Banjawarn, for example: its closest neighbor is 100 kilometers away, and its remote location made it the perfect home for Aum Shinrikyo, the Japanese doomsday cult allegedly responsible for a range of criminal and terrorist acts across the world. I remember hearing bits and pieces about them from my parents when we visited the station as kids, and feeling like I was staying on some cool movie set, complete with goodies and baddies and larger-than-life characters. Of course, Mum and Dad always kept the specifics from us kids back then. It was only when I grew up that I realized how bizarre this story is—so much so that it's put an eerie tinge on my favorite childhood destination. The outback is full of opportunities, some pure and some sinister; as the saying goes, "there's gold in them thar hills" but they are also full of secrets.

In 1993, Phyllis Thomas, who was from an Indigenous community close to Banjawarn, was with some other women when they
saw five men in a very remote part of the station. The men were
wearing helmets and full-length flight suits, and were standing next
to a twin-engine airplane. I can't imagine how strange it would have
been to see, living out in such a remote community in the desert. You
can go years on end in that part of Australia without seeing a soul,
so seeing oddly dressed men standing among the red dirt and grass
must have been an unearthly experience for them.

These men were a part of Aum Shinrikyo and had come to
Western Australia in search of areas suitable to mine uranium and
produce underground terrorist devices. The cult leader, Kiyohide
Hayakawa, personally visited the station during the search and even
noted the high quality of the ore there. It's crazy to think the place
we'd spend hours chasing cows and playing hide-and-seek in was
once inspected by a cult leader for uranium.

The cult traveled from Japan to Western Australia with
everything they needed to construct an underground bunker
and chemical warfare lab—from shovels to gas masks and liters of
harmful chemicals. Naturally, this conspicuously dodgy list of items
got the attention of customs officers, and the group was forced to pay
heavy import taxes and hand over their entire collection of chemicals
to authorities.

Still, the group managed to get the toxic ingredients and test
them on Australian soil. The cult sold the station in 1994; six months
later, cult members released toxic sarin gas into the subway system in
Tokyo—killing twelve people and injuring a whopping 1,000 more.
After the Federal Police figured out who had owned the station,

they went and examined the property. In a disturbing discovery, they found the cult's manmade bunker and sheep carcasses and soil containing traces of sarin gas. The terror attack completely rocked Japan, and it's weird to think of Banjawarn's connection to that.

If you ever visit a remote cattle station in Australia, you'll see why the cult chose one as their testing location. It's probably the same reason a dangerous in-patient from a psychiatric ward in Perth chose to flee to the station in the mid-2000s. This saga took place when Banjawarn Station's owner, Vicki, and her daughter, Jen, were alone on the homestead. They were down at the river behind the main house when, with no warning, a naked man appeared from behind some trees. For two women, this event alone would be scary enough—but the fact that they were in the middle of nowhere with no phone signal still gives me chills.

Fortunately, Vicki had her rifle on her and fired a couple of warning shots at the naked man, which was enough to scare him off, but who knows what would have happened if he had also been armed. The cops made the two-hour trip out to the homestead and came looking for him; they knew exactly who they were after. The naked man was a wanted and dangerous psychiatric hospital escapee who'd fled Perth on a freight train and jumped off on the station to hide.

I am glad my parents didn't tell me about that one until later in life, but it wasn't the last time I'd hear of spine-tingling encounters so far out bush. When I was around thirteen, my mum, aunties, and grandmother went on their annual girls' bush trip, camping about four hours out of Kalgoorlie in a very remote area of the Goldfields. I had school so I couldn't go—but I didn't need to be there for that trip to haunt me long afterward.

Mum is very experienced in the bush, along with the rest of my family, so they knew how to keep themselves safe. They had been at their camp for a couple of days without a single sign of another human being. Each day they'd leave camp to prospect, explore the ground by themselves, and just enjoy the experience, as they had on every other prospecting trip.

It was around three o'clock one afternoon when Mum stood up after going to the toilet and spotted a man no more than 50 meters from her. He was just watching, waiting quietly from behind a bush. Locking eyes with him sent shivers down my mother's spine. Once he knew he had been spotted, he ran for his car and took off. My mum called the other women to get back to camp. It's very fortunate a family friend was mining nearby and heard their conversation on the radio. He rushed to the location and made sure everyone was okay before searching for the man. He didn't find anyone. To this day we don't know who it was or what his intentions were, but it was intimidating enough to change my mum's sense of safety in the bush forever. This story is a little niche, but it's a universal experience: every woman has a story about when they feared for their personal safety.

Most of the time when I'm in the bush it's so relaxing. I have this sense of calm, knowing I'm all alone with no one else for hundreds and hundreds of kilometers. On the flipside, thinking you're all alone out there only to discover you have unexpected company shatters that tranquillity and preys on your mind forevermore. I struggled with that anxiety as a child, and it's stayed with me into adulthood. It's why I always have one eye open in the back of my head when I'm out bush. I know that's life—bad things can happen anywhere—but at least in the city, there's always someone to hear you scream.

When I meet someone new who lives in the bush, the thing I always analyze is why they're out here. Is it because they love the bush? Financial reasons? On-the-run reasons? Hiding reasons? I totally get living in the bush, it's beautiful, but it's surprising how many people live in the bush because they must—not because they want to.

Some people, like our mate Burkey, are way over on the want-to end of the spectrum. He is a lone prospector who has lived out of a caravan in the bush his whole life. He loves solitude, mostly hates people, and finds pure joy in being alone hunting for gold. You couldn't pay him to live in town. Most gold prospectors are like this—to do this job full-time you must love being alone in the bush and have some sort of desire to disconnect from society. Some people, like me, love a balance between that and living in the real world, but I totally get people who, like Burkey, love just existing in their little world out in the desert.

The people who I find the most interesting are the ones on the other end of the spectrum: the have-to end. I can't count how many times I have heard, "Oh, I think those people camped out over there don't want to be found," or something along those lines. I don't think the average Australian realizes that there is a whole population of people with a million reasons to escape society living in our remote outback.

One story that has always stayed in the back of my mind is that of a family living in the Murchison outback. The Murchison is rough terrain: the horizon is scattered with short shrubs, breakaways, cattle stations, red gravel, and thousands of kilometers between any signs of human occupation or sources of shade. It's a very hard area to stay alive in during the summer if you don't have the right set-up or knowledge. It's one of the last stops on Shit Creek I would want to be stuck at without a paddle.

When I was in my early twenties, Reece and I were camping with some friends about 60 kilometers north of Leonora on Kuwarra land, sitting around the fire at night chatting about who found the most that day and the plan for the next. I was eating my cold vegan mac and cheese—I couldn't be bothered cooking—when my mate John, whose lease we were on, turned to me and said, "Do you know who David Smith is?"

That's not his real name, but we'll run with it. I said I hadn't heard of him and asked why he wanted to know, and John went on to explain that David and his family were camped about 50 meters away. Reece had seen the family of three kids and their two parents walk past our swags that day with a wheelbarrow, some picks, and a small metal detector—a strange sight in the middle of nowhere. Reece had said to me that they were weird, but I just responded, "Reece, you think everyone is weird. They're probably just here to prospect with John on his lease."

John barely knew them when he got a phone call from David, desperately seeking help. His car had blown up halfway between Yalgoo and Leonora and he was stuck with his three kids, a dog, and a wife at a bus stop in the middle of nowhere. John couldn't get to them for another three days, so David had no choice but to camp out exactly where the car had broken down—a good example of why we always carry an extra five days' water and food when traveling in remote Australia.

John finally got him towed all the way into his camp past Leonora. He might have barely known David, but there is an unspoken code of mateship in the bush. You always help when needed, because you never know when you'll be the one needing the help.

John told me that there was something off as soon as he spoke to David and his family. The wife didn't speak much, whereas the kids all spoke as if they were in kindergarten, very underdeveloped and broken, even though they would have been young teens by then. The family had always lived in the bush year-round, but not in permanent camps or freehold houses—not even a caravan. They lived in tents.

As someone who has spent a lot of her life in the bush, I can appreciate the pros of this lifestyle—but I can also see the cons these kids would have had on the harder days: continuous 100-degree weeks with no air conditioning, no shower, and no escape, flipped to freezing winter nights in the desert with no heating. It would have been a tough upbringing. David also told John that at one point they lived in a big bus with twenty dogs. Apparently, all dogs ended up going "missing." I don't know what would make that story more bizarre—if it was real or fake.

I asked John why the Smiths were walking through the bush with a wheelbarrow, a pick, and their dog. Apparently, they were digging out an old-timer's shaft to follow the east–west vein. The north–south veins are the gold producing ones in those goldfields, but David didn't listen when John tried to explain this to him. John also tried to explain that the dog should not have been out there; this area was scattered with 1080 poison baits because of the huge wild dog problem, but, again, David didn't listen. I'd be surprised if the dog made it longer than a week. That's why we don't take our dogs out bush—that and they attract packs of wild dogs into camp.

David told John that the kids had never been to school, nor were they home schooled, hence the children's speech impediments. That also explained why they could barely read or write. John explained that they also lived off two-minute noodles and canned soup.

It takes more than hard work and dedication to succeed in life. People born into poverty often contend with intergenerational trauma, family instability, mental health issues, location setbacks, poor social skills, lack of education, confidence, and opportunity, and a plethora of other hurdles that kids like the Smiths' must overcome to break the poverty cycle. We open a whole new can of worms when we take into account the insane systematic racism in this country that nonwhite Australians deal with.

Even if these kids had left their family and gone out on their own, they would have had so many more obstacles to jump over than I ever did. This is one reason I will never attribute my successes just to hard work; it will always be my many privileges that got me to where I am, with some hard work along the way.

Another heartbreaking detail: even though John heard from someone else that David had five children, there were two girls missing. John asked David where the other girls went, and he replied, "We don't speak about those two anymore." A concerning response to say the least. By this point I was sitting in my camp chair, thoroughly freaked out to think about the family camping so close to us and questioning why I didn't just stay at home and watch Netflix.

John went on to tell us many bizarre stories about David that didn't make any sense. David had mentioned to John that he had a brain injury and sometimes forgot things he said. One night John heard blood-curdling screaming and horrific crying coming from the Smiths' camp. I am just glad I didn't hear that, because I can guarantee I would have been a mess. David came to camp the next day and said that his wife was "scratched on the face by the dog" the night prior, and was too embarrassed to come down to see everyone for the morning campfire and coffee. A friend who worked at Coles had also seen one of David's daughters try to run away from her father in town, begging strangers not to let him take her.

There were obviously a lot of unusual factors contributing to David's family's circumstances. It's a family that has stuck somewhere in my mind, and I often regret not ringing the police or child protection—or anyone. Mateship is so important in the bush, but it is very much defined by traditional masculinity. Of course it's instinctual to want to help vulnerable people, but it would have been taboo to intervene with David's personal business, even though we suspected he was hurting his wife and kids.

Growing up, I learned from the examples around me that straight white men were at the top of the food chain and standing up against them was a big deal. I felt below David, and I didn't feel comfortable going against him—and it seems the people around me felt the same. No one stepped in to protect that family. I think if it had been a mother mistreating her children with no man in the picture, the outcome would have been different.

I love the bush so much, but it can be isolating if you are stuck out there. I still feel horrible that those kids and that woman were stuck with David in the bush, with nowhere to go and no way of escaping—and that I turned a blind eye. I often get stuck in the moral grey area between minding my business, like I was taught, and standing up to oppressors. I am a big believer that if you silently witness oppression, you are just as guilty as the oppressor.

I never spoke to the Smiths, and I'd only pieced together the abuse story from what I had heard; I had no concrete proof that the kids or wife were in harm's way. They could have loved their life out there—but one phone call to the police could have confirmed that, or it could have saved them if something sinister was happening.

I learned from this situation that saying "Well, we don't know for sure" is a cop-out. Who really wins in a world where we mind our own business no matter the cost? I always strive to be a voice for the voiceless, and that time I made a bad call.

A couple of other people around the campfire told me how uneasy David made them feel, how his mere presence was off-putting. *And we're camped 50 meters away—how great!* I thought. I mentioned to the other campers that I was nervous to sleep in my swag so close to this man. The men's collective response was so predictable I could have bet my life savings on it: "You'll be alright." The women, meanwhile, all said some variation of: "Yeah, I would be a little nervous too."

It's interesting to me how men struggle to acknowledge that they walk through the world differently, and that they generally fail to consider women's lived experience. Women are much more likely to be sexually assaulted than men, and in this specific situation, it's a safe bet to say I would be an easier target for sexual violence than my male friends. Is it any wonder I find the "You'll be alright" response so invalidating? It did nothing to ease my mind; if anything, it made me feel silly for being afraid in the first place. Statistically, I was in more danger than the men who brushed off my worries and it goes to show they couldn't put themselves in my shoes. It's apples and oranges to us women, yet less obvious to men.

I'm sure it's not always deliberately dismissive. I think sometimes it stems from men wanting to reassure me that they will be there to protect me. The "You'll be alright . . ." might actually have the unspoken follow-up ". . . because I am sleeping just around the corner." They think I don't have to worry because I have a big tough man nearby. It would be nice if instead of a big strong man to protect me, we lived in a world where I didn't need one.

I might have been fine that night, but women know it's all too easy to become another stat on the list. In a world where one in five women is a victim of rape, we do not have time to trust everyone or differentiate the good from the bad. We only have time to assume the worst and act accordingly.

You ask any farmer or station hand, and they will tell you their number-one rule is this: don't fuck with the rain gauge. It's especially important to not fuck with it if the year is 2008 and you're on a remote station in far-flung desert with no internet or fancy app to tell you how much rain you've had.

I learned this lesson the hard way when one day, once again, I thought I knew better than everyone else (a character flaw I'm still working on as an adult): I decided to take the funnel out of the rain gauge because I thought it would catch more rain. The actual result: an inaccurate rain reading. Some would say it's common sense, something which thirteen-year-old Tyler lacked.

When some of the station owners checked the gauge, they couldn't tell how much rain we'd had overnight. They decided to risk it and set off on the three-hour trip into town, only to get very badly bogged halfway there. This had a domino effect—the rescue operation required extra hands, meaning that the station workers were too busy to start mustering cattle on time. One silly little mistake made by me meant a whole station couldn't start mustering when they needed to—and all station folk will know what a big mistake that is.

I could sit here now and write about the value of accountability—of owning your mistakes and making amends—but I'd be a phoney. What actually happened is that I lied to everyone and said it wasn't me who touched the rain gauge. So, if you're reading this, Mum and Dad, I'm sorry. I never touched the rain gauge again after that, I promise.

Station life is tough. You have to learn quick or learn hard—and, unfortunately for me, as a kid I formed a habit of learning hard. Dad always said, "If you're going to be dumb you need to be tough": basically, if you're going to fuck up you need to cop the consequences. For example, Colin Day, the other owner of Banjawarn and a very experienced bushman, always told us not to muster on a cloudy day; when I was about fifteen, I got to learn why.

In my sixteen years of prospecting I have had a few close calls, but there was only one time I was genuinely worried for my life. When we were kids, we never carried two-way radios or a GPS—firstly, because we didn't know how to use a GPS, and secondly, because we always accidentally went further than we were allowed, so we were always underprepared.

It was the July school holidays and I was with my extended family on our annual prospecting trip, camping on Wongatha land. It was a cloudy day, and the parents were out prospecting. My cousins, Reece, and I decided to ride the motorbikes 10 kilometers north to our friend's camp for pancakes. This sort of thing was a regular occurrence, except the pancakes were a treat. We told the mums that we were heading out and set off on our way. Reece and my cousin Jaxon, both twelve years old, took one bike; I took the other with my younger cousins Tatum and Demi, who were ten and eight years old, respectively.

When the boys said they bet I didn't know the way, I obviously replied, "Yes, I do," with total confidence. Of course I didn't—that was my first mistake, and a typical Tyler move. The boys wanted to make a point, so they took off too fast for us to follow them. Tatum, Demi, and I had got about halfway when the motorbike stopped dead in its tracks on an unused dirt path (that should have been the first clue that we were not where we were meant to be) and I realized my second mistake: I hadn't checked the fuel tank before we left.

We were all out, and in the middle of nowhere. I estimated that we were closer to our friend's camp than our own, so I then made my third mistake: we left the bike to follow the old track to our friend's camp on foot. Panic is a weird thing. In moments when you need to be your most rational, it seems you are your least.

The day before, a friend from another camp had conveniently dropped in to let us know that they had come across a lot of tracks and some big Alsatians, more than usual. He told my parents to keep us close to camp and to take the normal wild dog precautions: not leaving rubbish lying around, going to the toilet a fair way from camp, not taking pet dogs out bush, and so on. Even more conveniently, little Tatum and Demi had overheard this conversation—so when the bike stopped out in the middle of nowhere, their minds went straight to death by wild dog. I will always be more scared of wild dogs than any snake or spider, especially if they are in a pack. Dingoes are calm, timid animals, but when they crossbreed with feral dogs it's a whole new ball game. They have a strong pack mentality, making them very brazen and aggressive when there are three or more hunting together . . . and because food can be scarce, they are *constantly* hunting. They aren't wary of humans like dingoes; some wild dogs come from remote communities and breed there, meaning they associate humans and their camps with food.

Colin Day never mustered when the sky was cloudy because the sun is a very important navigational tool, and without it, it's very hard to orientate yourself. I never thought much of Colin Day's advice as a child because I wasn't going to ever muster cattle, obviously. Little did I know, it was some of the best bushman's advice I would receive—along with the very important "if you're lost, stay put and don't move" (which I was also about to learn the hard way).

So there I was: lost in the middle of the bush, responsible for my two younger cousins' safety, with no water and no idea. Then, about an hour and a half into our walk, the track we were following came to a stop. My heart completely sank. The trees looked different, the ground was unrecognizable, and Demi was crying.

To top it off, by this point I was carrying Demi on my back while Tatum hung off my right arm; they both swore that they had seen a wild dog in the distance. I was just trying to stay outwardly calm while inwardly deciding which of them I would sacrifice first. I made the call to retrace our steps back to the bikes, but I'd lost all sense of direction. It was a sharp panic I had never felt before. The old bush track we were on looked like it hadn't been used in ten years. I felt sick to my stomach about the danger I had put my younger cousins in and how much trouble I'd get into, but I was the most worried about not finding camp before nightfall.

After about five hours of wandering around the outback, we finally reached a track that looked like it *had* been used in the past decade. Better yet, it looked familiar; I spotted a fallen tree trunk that we'd had to drive around earlier. If that fallen tree wasn't there, I'm sure I would have walked the other way.

I felt a weight lift off my shoulders. We were safe. When we finally got back into camp, we all just cried. The boys hadn't even realized we were gone, and the parents had just assumed we were off doing our own thing. I was baffled that they had no idea we nearly died.

I said to Dad, "I thought we were going to have to spend the night alone and be mauled by a pack of fucking wild dogs!"

He just laughed and replied, "Well, I hope you learned a couple of fucking lessons."

Those two motorbikes feature heavily in stories from those trips. None of us cousins had really got into finding gold ourselves yet, so while our parents were prospecting we had to make our own fun. Our favorite game was Ultimate Hide-and-seek and we had two versions: one where the team that was "it" rode the two bikes while the hiders were on foot, and another version with both teams on a bike.

We made sure we were far enough from camp that our parents couldn't hear us breaking their 15-kilometer speed limit—which, in our defense, was not very realistic of them. We would hear often of station and farm accidents growing up—kids dying in motorbike accidents, getting horrifically injured playing in mineshafts and many other horrible stories. Despite this, we were young and dumb; we never wore helmets, constantly wandered off in the bush, often screamed around the outback in beat-up cars with no seatbelts and regularly played in old mines. The only reason it was never any of us who got hurt was pure luck. Now it truly terrifies me to look back on the things we used to do with no helmet and zero safety gear. We only had to make two emergency hospital trips because of the motorbikes. It's a miracle it wasn't more.

The first time, us kids and my uncle were flying kites on top of a hill when we decided to head back to camp for lunch. My uncle was in his car, the boys were on one motorbike, and Tatum and I were on the other—all without a helmet in sight. My uncle's parting words to us: "Do not race back." Naturally, we all decided to race back.

The boys were ahead and, not liking to lose, I decided to cut through a section of the bush they were avoiding (for good reason, I soon learned). Within a millisecond I'd driven the bike, and us, straight off a bank and into a meter-deep dried-out creek bed. Tatum hit the back of my head as she was thrown from the bike. My face smashed against the handlebars and two old rogue nails sticking off the top of the seat tore into my legs. I found Tatum and she was fine, but my face was bleeding, my legs were cut up, and I couldn't see straight. My uncle was furious and gave the boys a good talking-to before chucking me in the car and heading to hospital, 360 kilometers away. A broken nose and two cleaned-up wounds later, we were all banned from riding the bikes without helmets. I think that lasted a week.

The second trip to emergency featured many of the same ingredients. It was another motorbike accident at around the same age: Reece was thirteen and I was fifteen. We were with our parents about 300 kilometers out of Leonora on a prospecting trip. I was sitting in a creek bed and smashing up some quartz when it happened: I heard a huge *bang* and Reece screaming at the top of his lungs. My heart sank and I knew it was a motorbike accident.

Mum and I ran over to Reece, who was writhing in pain and stuck under the fence, with his Peewee 70 on its side 5 meters away. Reece had taken the corner too fast and slid off the bike straight into a star picket. It had pierced straight through his left leg, and it was a miracle he was wearing a helmet that day.

Like the time I broke my arm out on the station, Mum and Dad had to weigh up if Reece's injury was worth the six-hour round trip to Leonora. Only this time, they were pulling out gold left, right, and center on a massive patch. We really needed it and they had only worked half the area so far.

One parent could do the drive and one could stay and work the patch, but Reece's cut was deep enough that Dad was worried he would be transferred to Kalgoorlie; with only one car between the four of us, it wasn't really an option. We decided we'd all leave and just hope the patch wasn't raided before we returned.

We all made the trip to Leonora and Reece was stitched up at the hospital. Afterward, Mum and Dad decided we had just enough time to get back to the patch and smash out the rest of it before heading home. I remember clear as day Dad just yelling, "CUNTS!" when we made it back out there and he spotted the patch from the car. We were only gone forty-eight hours, but I knew immediately it had been raided.

The poachers might have got lucky and stumbled upon our abandoned patch, then decided to finish it off—which is fair enough. The patch was on pending ground and open to anyone, so technically the poachers hadn't done anything illegal. Of course, they might have been watching us work and waiting us out— another reason I feel unsafe in the bush sometimes. Even though we are in such a remote place, the possibility of being watched for your gold is very real. It's very easy to tell a gold patch: aside from the telltale tracks leading right into it, there are holes everywhere. We always fill our holes in after we're done, but you can still see where they were when the ground is freshly turned.

We went straight home after that. I realized that even though it was an accident, Reece's reckless behavior had cost Mum and Dad gold. That was our livelihood—although Dad was still working at the manufacturing plant at that stage, he had taken time off without pay for that trip, so it was a big loss. No pay and no gold meant living off two-minute noodles and bread. It was about survival at this point in our lives; we didn't have much money, so every last bit counted. Another bush lesson I learned the hard way.

These family trips continued throughout our childhood. We went on the first one when I was around nine, and our most recent one when I was twenty-three. Of all the places we've journeyed to, I've always loved visiting Sandstone. Over the years it's become a second home, and it's where my great-grandfather Ned spent a lot of time prospecting. There's even a photo of him in Sandstone's 100-year-old pub.

To give you a visual sense of where Sandstone is, it's *really* in the middle of nowhere in the Western Australian Murchison region. The closest major town is Kalgoorlie, and even that's 500 kilometers away. Sandstone is characterized by endless bright red hues, dramatic ranges, thick mulga trees, dried creek beds, and laterite hills. The town itself has a population of around fifty, but it's the cleanest and most cared-for Australian country town I have ever seen—and I've been to hundreds.

The closest police station and doctors are over 100 kilometers away—so if something goes wrong out there, you're in hot water. The Royal Flying Doctor Service is your only hope of getting emergency medical help, and you'd better pray reception pulls through to even call them in the first place. One snake bite in the bush when you aren't at camp, and you have a very slim chance of survival.

Sandstone itself is made up of a caravan park, a visitor center, a post office (only open twice a week), Black Ranges Café (which is only open in the winter, but they grow all their own produce—a real oasis in the desert,) and a pub that has a small grocery store attached. Sandstone also has a primary school that was abandoned when the last mine site closed and all the families left the town.

Once when I was around fifteen and we were camping in Sandstone, we found ourselves with a spare two-seater 1995 Hilux ute on our hands. It was old and looked like it belonged in the parts yard, but it was great because us kids got to drive it from camp and go exploring.

Us three girls were always in the tray, and the boys always drove—meaning they were on music duty. We had one CD in that car, and of course, it was the great old Kevin Bloody Wilson. Only two songs worked, so stuck on replay were "DILLIGAF" and "Absolute Cunt of a Day." Imagine an old ute screaming around the bush with three kids in the tray, a thirteen-year-old boy driving, and Kevin Bloody Wilson blaring from the radio. We would have looked like a bunch of unclaimed feral children.

There are two tourist sites in Sandstone: London Bridge and The Brewery. London Bridge is a natural sandstone bridge connecting two ridges, great for photos, and The Brewery is a great piece of gold rush history. In the early 1900s, Irishman JV Kearney wanted to provide booze for the many miners and prospectors working the area; he built The Brewery into the side of a breakaway on top of a 12-meter cliff, and used a combination of wells and gravity to make the beer—quite a remarkable operation. The Brewery once sold beer to surrounding hotels, but was forced to close when the railway line opened and Sandstone saw an influx of competing beer brands from elsewhere.

We used to drive the old ute to these two spots during peak visiting time to try to confuse tourists. We'd find it hilarious to rock up with Kevin Bloody Wilson blasting "C.U.N.T." from the speakers, us five filthy kids bouncing around in our beat-up old ute. The looks on the grey nomads' faces were priceless. The boys would rip the handbrake and do doughies before screaming off, leaving them all in a cloud of dust. I don't know why exactly we found that so entertaining, but I think part of it was that we could be little shits with zero consequences. Mum has always cautioned me about starting trouble because no matter where you are, you never know who's watching. I clearly never took her seriously.

On the same trip, us kids would drive the quad bike and the ute to the pub in town for a hot dinner and a proper shower. It didn't matter that the boys were thirteen and driving the car, or that us three girls were squeezed on a single-seater motorbike with no helmets—there were no cops around. We used to drive the quad straight up to the pub's front door, head in and have our shower, savoring every drop, even though our parents would mock us.

"You are all getting weak! Call yourself bush kids, driving into town to get a cooked meal and a shower!"

"You lot aren't camping; you're glamping."

We didn't give a shit. We were just stoked to get some beef-and-gravy rolls and wash our hair. It was a huge treat. We thought it was the best.

One night we rocked up at the pub looking like a bunch of degenerates, and as usual every patron turned our way and stared, trying to figure out where we'd come from and who we belonged to. I made sure all the kids kept their mouths shut and didn't answer any questions. Like any country town, Sandstone was full of lovely locals, but being the oldest cousin I felt responsible for the others and was always cautious.

On this night an old bloke who looked like he had crawled out of 1905 pointed at Jaxon and yelled from the other side of the bar, "You're a bloody O'Driscoll!"

The O'Driscolls are a well-known farming family in the Wheatbelt, and Jaxon and my other cousins are indeed part of the clan. We all froze, trying to figure out how the hell this guy,

700 kilometers away from home, knew who we were.

The guy then added, "I know your Pop and met you as a kid." We all were much more careful about how we acted after that. I guess Mum was right.

Sandstone really *was* like glamping for us; not only did we get beef-and-gravy rolls and a shower, but every single day around lunchtime us kids would also do the twenty-minute drive into town to visit Lady Di for her famous pies. I don't know if it was because we were camping in the middle of nowhere or because Lady Di's pies were genuinely amazing, but they were up there with the best foods I had ever eaten in my life.

Lady Di had a little roadside stall set up in Sandstone, and she always had a queue of people lining up for her food. Granted, most of her customers were grey nomads, but it was still impressive in a town with a population of fifty. She was an extroverted, out-there, larger-than-life character who I remember looking like Susan Boyle. She would have her little tarp and pie cooker ready to go; the delicious pies themselves were made to order. If you asked Lady Di what made her pies so famous, she would tell you it was her secret spice mix, which you could also purchase in a little sandwich bag. Every pie was truly delicious.

One day as I was putting that spice mix on some baked beans back at camp, I had my second million-dollar idea. My first million-dollar idea: when I was eleven, I made "perfume" from water and rose petals and sprayed Impulse deodorant in it before I sealed the lid. Genius. I sold it out the front of my house for $5 a bottle to neighbors and my parents. I made $40! I ended up donating it all to the RSPCA, but the fact remains—eleven-year-old Tyler could hustle.

This next big idea was to sell Lady Di's famous spice mix wholesale. It tasted great, it was versatile, and I could already see myself dazzling buyers with my amazing marketing pitch. I told Mum and Dad, who thought it was a great idea (lucky, because I was planning on asking them to cover the initial cost) and then wrote down a list of prospective merchants and approached Lady Di the next day.

When I get an idea like this, it happens so hard and fast that it consumes me. Even at that young age, all I could think about was executing that idea and doing so as soon as possible. My mind becomes a hive of questions. What will I do with the profits? How will I expand the business? How many sales can I make a month? There really is nothing that can come between me and making it happen. It's a good mindset for the most part, but also has its consequences.

The night before I pitched to Lady Di, I wrote lists upon lists about anything and everything to do with my new business venture, and anyone who had anything negative to say would infuriate me. Years later, when I received a life-changing mental health diagnosis, this intense irritability would make much more sense—but I guess it's hard to tell the difference between the normal mood swings that all fifteen-year-olds experience and something more sinister.

The next day I went to Di with my business pitch and she loved it! She even said she would give me her secret spice mixture. I was stoked. Then everything came to a screeching halt when Lady Di's whole pie operation was shut down by the health department—apparently a tarp shed and a pie maker on the side of the road aren't up to Australian health standards.

When I learned from one of Dad's mates what had happened, I was disheartened. The mate wasn't surprised; apparently Lady Di had got him to buy some mince from Kalgoorlie the week prior, telling him to "just buy the cheapest shit you can find; the tourists will never know." We all sighed in unison and decided home-made toasted sandwiches over the fire were a better lunch option anyway. I forgot about my million-dollar spice venture quickly after that.

I started to get the gold bug when I was around fifteen; one day I found a decent 5-gram nugget all by myself, about a meter away from Dad. The nugget was tucked under a saltbush—he had just missed it, and I still hold this over him today.

It was the best feeling—like winning the lottery without having to pay for a ticket. The emotional high was so exciting to me, and I was hooked. On prospecting trips, I began spending hours each day searching for gold. Every time I found a piece, I felt the little high all over again. I began to listen to my parents and wanted to understand how to read the land. I loved learning about all the geology, history, and indicators of gold.

My parents have always said that there is a difference between a prospector and a metal detectorist. A metal detectorist just picks up a detector and walks; a prospector reads the ground, follows a source, and knows the best way to extract the gold. Every time my parents had a prospector over for coffee or one stopped by at the camp, I would listen and learn from them. I realized early on that the best way to learn about prospecting is to listen to prospectors with experience. There were so many amazing stories and interesting little bits of information that I started writing them all in a journal.

Every night on our family trips we would sit around the fire, searching the sky for shooting stars and satellites. The one who spotted the most would be the winner, a good omen that usually meant they would find the biggest nugget the next day. Mum must have spotted a whole galaxy one night, because the next day she found a honey hole. That's our name for a minireef—a hole filled with gold fines, nuggets, and specimens. It was a rainy afternoon, and us kids were playing Ultimate Hide-and-seek with the quad bikes when Mum came into camp with a huge smile on her face and told us to follow her. She called the three adults over on the two-way radio, to which Dad said, in true Dad style, "It better be worth the walk." Mum promised it would be.

About 500 meters from camp, she had a very, very faint target she'd decided to dig. One thing Mum is good at is not missing even the slightest of targets—and her instinct was spot-on. It was a really good day.

A honey hole is a gold source, meaning that as we kept digging, the gold kept coming. The gold was all in a quartz vein and we were taking coolers full of gold-bearing ore at a time. All of us kids—the cousins, Reece, and me—sat around the hole, pulling quartz chunks out in the rain, and transporting the full coolers on the quads back to camp just over the hill.

It was pouring rain, but we all celebrated into the night; the parents drank beer while us kids stayed up later than usual, enjoying their good spirits.

The adults continued drinking and Dad managed to score some fireworks (illegal, yes, but he was very safe) and we spent an hour setting them off into the night sky. Us kids thought it was the best night ever. I still remember Dad shooting them off into the stars, miles and miles away from any other people.

We ended up getting 40 ounces out of Mum's honey hole. When I ask her now what she loved so much about that moment, she always says, "Watching you kids get to enjoy gold with me."

The best bit for me: for the first time I felt like a *real* prospector getting to help. It's always been one of my favorite memories. It's still my dream to find a source like my parents have done so many times. Hopefully one day I will.

6

CATCHING GOLD FEVER

My parents were very lenient with me while I worked at the gold shop. We still laugh about how easy I had it. On school holidays I would work there for a weekly wage, but most days I would have my hour-long afternoon nap around 3 p.m. and take money out of the till for my lunch. I would also leave the shop altogether whenever I wanted to see a movie with my mates, and sometimes even take money out of the till to buy clothes, then blame the missing $20 on Dad "forgetting" to put a receipt back in. It is funny to think about now, but I am aware of just how privileged I was.

I embarked on another great entrepreneurial venture in that job. I would crawl around on the floor near where Dad would smash up gold specimens, and use tweezers to pick the excess flecks of gold out of the cracks. I would spend hours doing this instead of serving customers. It makes you wonder why Mum and Dad kept Reece and me on.

To be fair, we did help with all the less desirable jobs, which lightened the workload for my parents. It would have been more economical to hire staff, but my parents refused—the only people they trusted were Reece and me. They made sure we understood that you couldn't trust anyone in the gold game.

For the seven years we owned that gold store, we never had any extreme security breaches. Obviously, our security was next level—security cameras, emergency buttons, a top-of-the-range alarm system, and a top-of-the-range safe—but I think we can also thank my parents' honest reputation and the respect they've earned in the gold community. When I was growing up, my parents drilled into me that all you have is your name—ruin that and you've fucked yourself. They really did stand by that, and it's made me a very proud daughter.

I rarely heard anyone disrespect my parents. The closest incident was the man who looked my mother dead in the eye during a gold deal and told her, "This place would be so easy to rob." He was very intimidating, and I can guarantee he wouldn't have said it if my father was there. Mum rang the gold police and handed over his details as soon as he left. He received a visit from the head of the gold squad, and we never saw him again.

I heard so many things as a child working in that store, but learned very quickly to keep my mouth shut and mind my own business. We would have so many customers coming in and blabbing about ripping people off, getting ripped off themselves, decades-long friendship breakdowns, marriage problems, money problems, car problems, bikie relations, drugs, guns, and—of course—sex.

As time went on, I learned very quickly that a lot of the gold world was underground, above the law, and truly a man's world. If you want to make it in gold, there is a unique set of rules that you must live by.

The two most important ones are keep your mouth shut and trust no one. These were very clear to me by the time I hit high school.

I was working the counter once when a lone full-time prospector came in. He told me that during the night, one of his mates had been stealing gold out of the vein they were mining together. The mate thought he was getting away with it, but in revenge the prospector went to their safe, stole the 14 kilograms of gold they had recovered together, and left with it all. On his way out he shot up the camp, and hadn't seen his "mate" since. I was fourteen and just awkwardly laughed before handing over his check.

Working in that store and growing up in the gold game really influenced my opinions and worldview. I began to see the power imbalances of the patriarchy playing out in day-to-day life. I saw how men treated my mother compared to my father, and I began to question why customers would refer to my father as the boss when Mum and Dad were equals who shared responsibility. Did Dad command more respect than Mum? If so, is this something that men and women are socialized to do differently, or was it just their personality types?

I developed a chip on my shoulder about constantly proving my knowledge to our older male customers. There were few people who respected my opinion without me having to prove myself first, which is somewhat understandable because of my age—but it became tiring. I noticed that Reece was given a spot at the table, no questions asked, while I had to beg just to stay in the room. I am so lucky that my parents backed me every single day; it made me believe that I can hold my own against anyone.

I worked in the shop with Mum and Dad, with Reece helping

sporadically on school holidays. Mum and Dad took care of the back end equally, and I dealt with the front end of the shop for the most part. This meant I would greet all the customers—90 percent were male—and process exactly what they needed. If they were there to sell gold, I would get Mum or Dad to take them to the back room where we did the deals.

As I got older my parents gave me more responsibility. I was allowed to buy gold under 20 grams, decide the price, grade the nuggets, and write the check without my parents' help. Keep in mind that by this point I had worked there a long time, so I had watched thousands of gold deals and sold as many ounces of gold. I was confident in my abilities and my parents were always on my team.

There is one encounter that has always stuck in my mind, and I feel it was a defining moment for my character. It was late afternoon when a middle-aged white man came into the store, saying he wanted to sell some gold. I said sure and asked to see it—and that's where it started to go downhill. He started to get a little irritated and asked if he could see the boss. I said they were both busy and it would be quicker if I saw the nugget so I could grade the gold.

With hesitation he showed me the "nugget," which was in fact pyrite, also known as fool's gold (the name is fitting here)—quite obviously not gold. I told him so and that went down like a lead sinker in a dam! He was certain that his valueless pyrite rock was real gold, and he was clearly not happy that a young woman was telling him he was wrong.

He swore at me for a while, hoping that might change the rock's chemical composition. When he tired of that, he demanded I fetch the "boss" to confirm it was a gold nugget. By this point I was a little rattled. It was quite intimidating having an angry man yelling at me. I think he was hoping that if he bullied me he would get what he wanted, and I guess it worked because I went and got Mum. Alas, he was not happy with Mum either and once again demanded to see the "boss."

"I know a man works here. I've seen him. I want to speak to him," he growled. Dad had heard what was happening but gave Mum and me the space to sort it ourselves; he knew we were capable. Even though that gesture may seem minor, it helped a lot. I ended up grabbing the rock and walking to the back to show Dad, who said, "Tell him it's obviously not a piece of gold and to get the fuck out of the store," so I did just that.

Two things happened that day: one man shrank my confidence, and one man restored it. Dad could have easily walked out there and taken care of the situation; it may have saved everyone some time, but it would have reinforced the idea that men respect the opinion of another man over that of a woman. While I know this to be generally true, little moments like that one have helped me develop the confidence to challenge these men.

If I bring up experiences like this with men, they often meet me with complaints about generalizing and insist that not all men are like that. Not all men are, but internalized misogyny often does play out on a subconscious level. It's something we all contend with; I often catch myself out doing the exact same thing. I reflect on my internalized misogyny quite often. I think self-reflection is extremely important, and we are not entitled to an opinion without self-awareness. I've come to realize one way I project my internalized misogyny is that I tend to question female experts while blindly believing male experts. Don't get me wrong—I believe it's important to ask questions, but it's equally important to hold men and women to the same standards.

Working in the gold shop gave me an intense and rare glimpse into the gold world. People who work in gold are usually loners and stick to themselves, which made my family members and me anomalies—we were super-social prospectors. Not to mention, as the only gold buyers in the Kalgoorlie/Murchison region, a lot of people relied on us. They treated us like family, and we often became their psychologists and banks—and sometimes we were the only real human contact they would have besides the cashier at Coles. Through the shop, we interacted with others in the field nonstop for seven years, giving us behind-the-scenes access to the lies, stealing, betrayals, and successes that go with that kind of work. We heard everything firsthand: where the big nuggets were coming from, who was finding them and who was stealing them. My parents would always tell me to listen with my ears shut. I guess that meant I was to forget everything that person had told me as soon as they left the store. There were a few times my parents retold stories outside the family, but it was very rare and usually because they were legally obligated to share information with the gold police. My parents didn't support the underworld by any means, but they were also very aware that their name was their name, and once that was tarnished it was almost impossible to restore.

One of the craziest people I met while working in my parents' gold shop was a man named Alex (we will call him that for the sake of his anonymity). This title is a big call because while working in that store, I met people from all walks of life; Alex is one I will never forget.

I first met Alex when I was sixteen. He would have been around forty, and used to come in with his wife and kids, who he lived with in the bush. They traveled between Western Australia and Queensland seasonally. Alex was a tall man with long hair, which he would wear in a low ponytail, and he was always covered in dirt. He was lovely, his wife was lovely, and so were his kids. There was just something a little strange about them, something that intrigued me. I have always been drawn to people and their stories.

I once said to Dad, "Alex is so nice."

"Yes," Dad replied. "But he's one man you shouldn't fuck with."

It was a surprising comment. I poked and prodded for more information and Dad said, "Tyler, he's fine when he is taking his meds but, Jesus, he has some demons when he isn't. I will always respect him, though, because he has always respected me." That's another thing I admire about my parents: they don't care what walk of life you come from—if you respect them, they always respect you.

I continued to try to get more information out of my parents about Alex and his family. I would listen carefully to conversations when they came in to sell gold, and I would eavesdrop when my parents talked about him. My parents rarely sheltered me from the outside world, but they were selective when it came to things that were simply none of my business, like Alex's past. His wife once brought in a short poem for my mum that was quite bizarre to say the least. It was about how much she liked Mum after they had met a couple of times; it was very sweet but a little strange.

Alex and his family were real modern-day wild westerners. I remember Alex once told me that they'd often pick up roadkill to eat because that's what his parents did, and his grandparents before that. "You cut off the bad bits and it's just like buying it from the shops," he said. I never judged him as I never knew his financial situation, but you must be a certain type of bush dweller to enjoy roadkill.

I eventually learned for myself why Dad had said Alex wasn't one to fuck with. One day, Alex told me about how he had shot up an elderly couple's caravan because they stole some gold from him. Alex told the story with the typical swearing and yelling, but from what I could gather he had found a rich patch and was working the ground. He left camp during the day and came back to notice an elderly couple camping about 800 meters away. They weren't camping on Alex's ground, but it was weird to see others camping so close in such a remote part of the outback.

The elderly couple said hello and had a quick chat, and Alex gave them the stay-away-from-our-ground spiel, which they seemed to accept. Alex had only worked about half the patch when he had to do the big drive into town again for supplies. He came back to realize his patch had been worked while he was gone—and whoever it was had found a lot of gold.

The only fresh tracks led to the couple camping over the hill. There were no other tracks in or out. Alex took off to see if he could catch them. He did; they were on the highway to a different town. Like something out of a movie, Alex got out his handgun and shot up the caravan *as they were driving*. He completely covered it with bullet holes, then did a U-turn and went back to camp.

The way Alex told the story was different—it was much more casual, like just a regular Sunday morning bakery run. It's funny; when Alex first told the story, I didn't really think he was in the wrong. I personally wouldn't have shot up a caravan, but I also wouldn't have stolen someone's gold. I guess that couple had caught gold fever.

Mum and Dad ended up explaining to me that Alex had schizophrenia and, at one point, had been on Australia's top ten most wanted list. This blew my mind. I had never felt scared in his presence. Come to think of it, I had been in the same room as many criminals before and rarely felt uncomfortable. I think people who grow up around criminal activity and people in low socioeconomic areas naturally develop a protective instinct for their communities.

This is a generalization, and of course I'm not glorifying criminals, but growing up around people like this really drilled in the importance of family and loyalty. Dad always said that if you needed $5000, you could ask one of his friends (whose background was similar to Alex's) and this friend would have it for you within the hour, no questions asked—but if you took $5000 from him, you were done. It was a sort of honor among thieves: an expectation that if you said you were going to do something, you did it: you didn't lie, didn't rip people off, and didn't sully your reputation. The world is a small place, and the gold world is smaller.

Gold prospecting in Australia was built on mateship. The gold world does get a bad rap sometimes, but at its core, it's a culture where if someone is your mate, you have their back to the end. This mindset is a beautiful thing that I respect so much. For the most part it is a world shaped by the understanding that you have your mate's back until he doesn't have yours. Prospectors have always understood that mateship means when it comes to survival, you look out for each other—although gold fever does get in the way.

This identity was forged in the gold rush days when mates toiled together in the harsh conditions of the outback. Back then, the mining could not be done alone. Digging 12-meter-deep shafts, living in 100-degree heat, and traveling hundreds of kilometers for water were all too dangerous to do without a mate.

Mates shared just about everything: food, water, earnings. Everything except for gold information. Once the mates went to war, this camaraderie took on another layer of meaning with the hardships the Anzacs endured. It remains a sacred part of who we are today.

One of the most publicized tragedies that happened while I worked in the gold store was the disappearance of the Kehlets in 2015. The Kehlets were announced missing after locals found their emaciated dog walking alone through Sandstone, which led to the biggest missing persons search in the state's history.

The dog had walked all the way into town, 25 kilometers away from where the Kehlets had been camping, which set off the alarm bells. I am also surprised it made it that far with the number of baits in that area. The huge investigation recovered the body of forty-seven-year-old Mr. Kehlet. They found him naked at the bottom of a 100-year-old abandoned mine shaft called the Bell Chambers shaft, only two kilometers from their camp. Even after a huge search effort (including scouring 100 more shafts) Mrs. Kehlet was never found.

I remember hearing about this when I was sixteen. At first, I thought it was a couple of prospectors who had broken down somewhere remote and that the search would be over in a couple of days. As the weeks went on, it became clear something more sinister was going on.

Working in the gold shop at the time, we heard rumors start to swirl. The gold game is very small. Incidents like this rattle a community; not only did it send fear into the hearts of people living in Sandstone, but it also shook gold prospectors around the country. It's one of those cases that have stayed with me since. It made me question my routines and second-guess decisions that were normally autonomous.

There is still a bounty out on Mrs. Kehlet's body. It's always in the back of my mind when I am prospecting in the outback. One of the suspects was a friend they were prospecting with at the time— someone they trusted, a brave thing to do in the gold world. It's rumored he murdered Mr. Kehlet, stole his gold, and took off with Mrs. Kehlet. Without her body they don't know if she is dead or alive. Of course, these are only small-town rumors. There has never been any proof.

I remember sitting in the Sandstone pub years later and overhearing some old locals discussing the case. They were drinking Emu Export, were covered in red dirt, and wearing clothes that could have passed for rags. They were telling the barmaid that they'd come across a man who matched the friend's description on an old dirt highway leaving Sandstone, all around the time of the incident.

The man was stopped on the side of the road, so they pulled over to see if he was okay. This is normal practice in the bush; you always check on people. As much as lying and stealing are rife, mateship is survival. Once they pulled over, the man yelled over at them to fuck off. They heard what they think was a woman's scream from the back of his car and the man became even angrier. Fearing for their safety, they took off, and then only reported it later once the story had been publicized. Again, small-town rumors—but enough to make the hairs on the back of your neck stand on end.

Stories like this are one of the reasons we only work with family, and why I am always watching over my shoulder out bush. We obviously take precautions, but I am sure the Kehlets (and all of the other prospectors who go missing in our goldfields every year) did as well.

I often speak to my father and other men about how it's intimidating to be in the bush as a female. Surprise, surprise—it's often met with the standard "you'll be alright." It makes me wonder what it would be like to live in a world where you're not constantly worried about being murdered by a man—one where you don't have to constantly look over your shoulder.

7

FOOL'S GOLD

My Pa would always say, "You don't get rich working for anybody else." I don't think when my Pa said this he realized that it would set the course for my career choices, but it did. It's something that I have thought about regularly since the day I first heard it.

The thing about working for someone else is that generally it caps your earning potential, and even as a child that annoyed me. I wanted my pay to reflect how hard I worked and how much I was hustling—not a set hourly rate. I have always been a hard worker, but as a child I was confused as to why you would work hard for someone else if they were going to pay you the same amount anyway. I have since learned that there are obvious flaws in that line of thinking, but it still cemented some deep beliefs in my young brain.

When I finished high school in 2012, I decided to have a gap year, as did most of my friends. Some of us were planning on staying in Kalgoorlie to work on the big mines, but my friends and I wanted to save money so we had some behind us for the following year, when we would move 600 kilometers away to Perth for college.

Looking back now, it's funny because saving money is the last thing I did. I worked with Mum and Dad at the gold shop and was paid $600 every Friday, but because I'd spend all my money on the weekend, I'd need a loan by Monday. By the time Friday came around I was in debt to them. On Fridays, when Mum would give me $600, I would also hand her back $150 for the car they bought me and then I would buy $100 in gold as my savings. This, on top of paying off my usual weekend debt to them, meant I'd be left with about $150—which would then take me three days to blow on festivals, partying, and clothes. My life consisted of partying, napping, eating, and sometimes sleeping; it was my last year of true freedom.

In August 2013, I met Max, an electrician who had moved from the other side of Australia as a teenager to work on the mines. I was seventeen and he was my first ever boyfriend. We moved quickly, and within two months he was living with me and my parents. Seventeen is such a tender age. We were still learning about who we were, what we liked, what we stood for, and who we wanted to become. Being in a serious, committed relationship at that age influences all of those things heavily.

Some people start dating the love of their life in their teenage years. They get lucky, grow with their partner, and are always on the same wavelength. All I cared about was that we had fun together. I guess that's what's important in your teenage years, but my teenage years quickly turned into my adult years and, before I knew it, I was in a relationship with someone on a completely different wavelength and no one had taught me how to say goodbye.

Another thing that happens when you begin a serious relationship at such a young age: you form immature habits that stick. I wish I'd known that these habits—the codependency, the emotional dependency, the insecurities—would last until we were twenty-three. At the time, I should have been learning to develop my own thoughts and feelings, and learning to find comfort alone. Not every young relationship is like this, and I wouldn't change anything because it really has made me who I am today, but if I could go back and tell seventeen-year-old Tyler anything it would be "do not lose yourself." Which I did.

When I was seventeen, my aunty bought me my first tattoo as an early eighteenth birthday present. I swore black and blue to my parents that I would never regret it, insisting it was a quote I had wanted for years. That was a flat-out lie: the night before on Pinterest, I had found a photo of the quote tattooed on a tan girl's skin and thought it looked cool. The tattoo I got on my ribs read: "Life is nothing more than a reflection of your state of mind." I don't even think I had the emotional intelligence to comprehend what that meant.

It was an impulse—the first of twenty-five (and growing) permanent impulses I have on my skin. People often ask me what my tattoos mean. They are mostly the result of a mixture of spontaneity, boredom, having an extra $100 in my wallet, adventures with friends, and moments when I managed to peer pressure a friend into a matching tattoo. Three or four hold actual personal significance, my favorites being my late friend Lucy's initials and a matching quote with my cousin Tatum.

You can't really read that first tattoo anymore; it was done by the local tattoo shop. Even if I did regret it, I would never admit it to anyone because I am too stubborn and, besides, it's all good for the plot.

By the time I turned eighteen, I'd well and truly caught gold fever. I prospected on weekends when I wasn't too hungover, and our annual prospecting trips with my cousins, the O'Driscolls, were the best part of the year and are by far my favorite memories. The O'Driscolls and my brother and I have such a strong bond that I will always be so grateful for. We are much more like siblings than cousins, and all of my best memories involve them. The bush trips we did together while our parents prospected for gold are priceless and I wouldn't swap them for the world. Though these trips were amazing, it was still a part of my identity I tried to hide. I was slightly embarrassed to be known as someone from the bush. I guess when you are a teenager, anything that doesn't fit the norm is embarrassing—tall poppy syndrome in full swing.

After years of being immersed in the gold game and not venturing far from the Goldfields, I began to feel stagnant, which to me feels like failure. It was a strange feeling to absolutely love prospecting, gold, and the life I lived there, and yet still resent so much of it.

I loved the slow pace and my comfort zone, but I felt a very strong urge to escape. When I finally moved to Perth to study social work, I transitioned into a new chapter of my life—which I see now as the moment my childhood really ended.

I left the bush armed with street smarts from working the gold shop, and countless lessons from my parents. I think my initiative came from watching Mum and Dad perform a million bush fixes; my imagination came from the thousands of hours spent making my own fun; my independence came from a free childhood roaming the outback. I have enjoyed so many privileges in my life and one of those is my childhood.

At this stage I didn't see gold prospecting as a career path I would follow. I loved it but only saw it as a hobby; I think I honestly didn't believe I could make it as a full-time prospector. I really wanted to help people, so I decided to study social work instead. I wanted to be involved with child protection specifically; growing up, I saw kids from less privileged backgrounds and I wanted to be part of dismantling the poverty cycle.

It still blows my mind that at seventeen we are expected to decide what career we want to follow for the rest of our lives. There was so much pressure after school to get a trade or a degree. Maybe it was because I was from the country, but it would have been very helpful for me to learn about alternative career pathways like creative ventures, or entrepreneurship.

While I studied, Max and I lived with my O'Driscoll cousins on my Aunty Sha and Uncle Damo's farm in Grass Valley, an hour and a half away from college. There have been a couple of times in my life when Max and I lived on that farm, our heads kept above water by Sha and Damo's generosity. They let us live there rent-free, fed us, and made us feel completely at home. They bent over backwards for us. Sha and Damo are exactly the kind of parents I want to be when I am older, and I will always be beyond thankful for what they have done for me.

I loved broadening my knowledge and learning about social work and psychology, but I loathed the structure of college itself. I really struggled learning in that environment. One of my lecturers once told me that I needed to significantly improve my writing skills if I wanted to go somewhere academically—ironic, considering I got a book deal seven years later.

I always received feedback that my content, and the thought behind it, was great, but my writing, grammar, and referencing skills weren't up to scratch. *Fuck this,* I thought to myself. *I don't learn like this.* So after only a year, I quit. Looking back, it was probably a bit lazy, and if I really wanted to be a social worker I should have knuckled down and learned to write in academic contexts. Instead, I decided to open my own jewelry business, Mae by Tyler.

We moved home to Kalgoorlie, where Max returned to his old job with a local electrician and I returned to work at my parents' shop. By this point they had sold it, though, so I worked with the new owners to help with the transition. It was also good for the customers to see a familiar face in the store; it helped them build trust in the new owners.

I learned the basics of jewelry making while working in the gold shop, and then I taught myself the rest from Google and YouTube. I spent hours researching it all. My parents had collected stones and silver during their time owning the shop, so I was very lucky to receive a big bundle of supplies from them to help me get started.

I worked on my jewelry business on the side, before and after work. This is when Max started withdrawing, missing work and sleeping and drinking a lot. He just became very sad. At the time I had no idea what was going on, but with hindsight I can say these were the first signs of depression. Every time I asked him what was wrong, he would say nothing and insist he was fine. I found it so frustrating. Something was clearly wrong, so why was he lying to me?

I spent hours on end trying to fix him and force him to speak to me. It's clear now that Max knew something was wrong, but didn't know what it was or how to explain it. My aversion to pain and vulnerability really made it hard for me to know how to help Max navigate those feelings. I was young and didn't know how to relate. I wish he knew back then that his pain didn't need to be logical or an obvious wound to be valid. The idea that pain must make sense or be physical for it to be real is poisonous.

I had never had a boyfriend before, let alone one with undiagnosed mental health conditions, so I had zero ideas about what a healthy relationship looked like. I started withdrawing from my friends to be with him and worried about how my future would look if that's what relationships were like. I went from a carefree seventeen-year-old soul, whose only worries revolved around ways to sneak into the pub, to a shadow of my teenage self, dealing with what felt like a doomed mission to try to make Max happy. It wasn't my job to fix him, but that's how it felt. I wish I could go back and tell younger Tyler that his happiness was not my daily responsibility.

When I was eighteen, I was driving to social netball one day when I received a text from him: "We need to talk when you get home." He had been very distant that whole day, so my mind went straight to assuming he had cheated on me—a selfish thought, maybe, but that's where my brain went. I could barely concentrate at netball, and I thought my heart was going to explode out of my chest. I got home and he was lying facedown in the pillows in complete darkness. My stomach just sank.

It took a lot of courage, but Max finally opened up about parts of his history that explained so much of his mental state. Not that you ever need a reason for a mental illness to manifest, but the trauma he went through when he was younger shone so much light on what was going on. I was the first person he had ever disclosed that information to, and I can't fathom it; it would be like poison slowly eating away at you every day. It was clear to me then that he had PTSD and needed professional help. It was the beginning of a monumental shift in our relationship, and the people we were each becoming.

Max began to do fly-in fly-out (FIFO) work on a four-and-one roster—four weeks away and one week home. Anyone who has done FIFO, or has had a partner doing FIFO, will understand why that roster is called "the widow maker."

Maintaining a healthy relationship when one of you is doing FIFO is hard work. It takes genuine trust, great communication skills, stable mental health, and solid financial goals—none of which we had. I had become extremely emotionally codependent, and lost my sense of self; it put a huge strain on our relationship.

As much as I loved Max, I truly wish we had gone our separate ways by that point. He would get upset if I hung out with my friends without him, so I stopped; he didn't like me getting tattoos because he thought it was a waste of money, so I didn't; I was always looking for validation from him to allow me to do things I wanted to do. My dependence on him was holding me back from growing at an age when I should have been pouring energy into figuring out who I was, what I liked, and what I stood for.

Independence is a gift. It took me too long to learn that being lonely is a whole lot better than being with someone who isn't the right person. It also took me too long to learn that if you're scared of being alone, you will settle for anyone. I put up with too much unhappiness in that relationship because I had such a deep belief that being unhappy was better than being alone.

I don't have regrets—that relationship made me who I am and carried me to the person I am meant to be with—but if I could give advice to any seventeen-year-old out there who is caught up in finding a partner, it would be to invest that energy in yourself. Learn to love yourself. Learn what kind of person you are, where you want to live, and how you want to spend your money. Time will give you more than any partner will ever give you. Completely nail being alone before you even consider putting energy into a relationship. Once you have found peace alone, the person who is meant for you will turn up—and if they turn out to not be the right one, then you will have the resources and strength to say goodbye and wait for someone better.

When you're seventeen, the traits you are looking for in a partner are generally superficial—which is fine for a bit of fun, but not an ideal start point for launching into a committed relationship. When I met Max, I loved that he liked me back, played footy, was a tradie, worked out, and wanted to travel. No one tells you this, but I wish I had asked Max the important questions before I got into a committed relationship at that age. Who do you vote for? What are your values? What are your morals? Do you support the LGBTQI community?

What are your thoughts on racism? The answers to these are so important to me. But I didn't think of them at seventeen. I should have thought about his political views, money habits, and work ethic. I should have been discussing taboo subjects with him. I never imagined that I would be in a long-term relationship with someone who voted for a party whose values clash with my own—and it's a little harder to escape six years in than if you had just figured that out at the start.

I am now surrounded by people who are on the exact same page as me. I will never lose a friend or partner because I find out they are racist or homophobic, because I make sure to figure out their views before I get in too deep. I learned from Max that I don't have to sacrifice important parts of myself just to keep a relationship alive. I learned it was okay to let the relationship die, because new ones are born every day. Some relationships are worth fighting for and some simply are not.

Max was working away by this point, and I was still friends with all the girls I went to high school with. All we had in common was that we lived in the same town and we liked to party. Even then, I had such different beliefs, motivations, and morals from those friends'. We were always butting heads—and I find it hard to bite my tongue when it comes to disagreements.

I was sad when we started to drift, but I realized it wasn't worth holding on to something that made me so unhappy. Clinging to something because you put a lot of time into it isn't a good enough reason to keep it in your life. When I said goodbye to those seven-year friendships, it wasn't a waste. I quickly learned that life successes aren't always measured in hours; they are measured in lessons and shared moments.

Coming out of a codependent relationship has taught me just how important your friends are. Partners might come and go but your friends are your support network and will be the ones there for you through thick and thin. I was sad when I let go of my high school friendships, but it wasn't long before I found my people. I now have a close friendship group that is so important to me, just as important as family. These friendships are so worth putting time and effort into; I make a conscious effort to be with my close friends as much as I can because I will never let myself be so emotionally dependent on a partner again.

The friends that I lost taught me a lot of lessons—most importantly what I like in a friend and what I don't. They also gave me so many amazing memories that will never fade, regardless of the current status of that friendship. Holding on to those friendships would have been a disservice to myself as I grew into the person I am today. Sometimes the best thing you can do is say thank you and move on.

8

PANNING FOR GOLD OUT EAST

I once again found myself feeling stagnant. I was nineteen and hanging around those friends who I liked but I didn't feel were truly my people. Even though I was working at the gold shop and trying to get my jewelry brand off the ground while Max was away, I just felt so bored.

I started to feel anxious that I was wasting my life away, so I sent photos off to nine modeling agencies around Australia; modeling was something I'd always wanted to pursue. All of them said no except one: Chadwick in Melbourne. All the nos were disheartening but this one yes made up for it. The agent in Melbourne rang me to invite me in for a meeting the following week. When she asked me where I lived, I told her I was in Western Australia and she promptly said we couldn't take things further if I was interstate.

I lied on the spot: "Oh no, I live in Melbourne. I'm just visiting family, but I'll be back in two weeks." Just like that, I had two tiny weeks to move my whole life to Melbourne, figure out what Max and

I would do and explain to my family that I was leaving. I believe "oh wells" are better than "what ifs," and I always walk through doors when they open for me and figure out the rest later.

Impulsiveness and a lack of understanding of consequences have wreaked havoc in my life, but they have also brought me great joy. This time, those traits empowered me to move my whole life across the country for a meeting with a modeling agency at nineteen, but they've also cost me a lot in years since. Now I can see that the reason I could make that decision on the spot wasn't bravery or wisdom; it was the first symptom of my mental illness.

I rang Max and said, "I have a meeting with a modeling agency. I'm moving to Melbourne."

"I'm coming with you," he replied.

Tick—that was the first job done. Next, I told my parents, and they were over the moon for me. I can always count on total support from them; they have never held me back from my goals. They have not only pushed me to follow my dreams, but have also made it very clear that they will be there to catch me if it doesn't work out. I was never scared of my Melbourne plan failing, because I knew I could just come back to Mum and Dad. This is truly a privilege; it's easy not to fear failure when failure looks like pure love and acceptance.

I had two weeks to find a rental in Melbourne with no family, friends or even acquaintances to do a rental inspection for me. I had to find a private rental on Gumtree. It might have been smarter to book an Airbnb for a month and then find a secure rental once we got to Melbourne, but I was nineteen and didn't think my plan had any blind spots. I found a rental on Gumtree, and sent the bond and the first two weeks of rent to the bank account of a stranger from the internet. Nineteen-year-old me didn't see a problem with this and I promised Max we would have a house to move into when we got to Melbourne.

The next problem I had to figure out was money. After sending rent and bond funds, I had $800 left in my bank account to move my whole life over to Melbourne. I also didn't have a job lined up when I arrived, so I decided I would need more than the $800—smart thinking, Tyler.

The combination of my poor grasp of consequences and my impulsive spending sprees has always been an issue for me. This came into play when the Kalgoorlie races were held the week before we were due to leave; I bought a new dress and shoes, and spent about $200 on booze. My bank account was looking very thin. I then decided to bet $100 on a horse race, which was basically the last of my money.

I don't know if this was extremely reckless, spending all my money before I moved to the other side of the country, or if it showcased my optimism that it would all just work out. I still struggle with this today—when making decisions, I always walk the line between trusting that the universe will have my back and making outright irresponsible choices. I can rationalize almost everything. If I were to crash my car, it wouldn't upset me because I'd know I could just get it fixed and in a year's time it wouldn't matter. I guess this kind of thinking has perks, but I also think it is a trauma response. Sometimes I would have such bad anxiety around Max that the only thing that calmed me down was to repeat to myself, "If it won't matter in a year, it shouldn't stress me now." This mentality means that I could, and still can, dissociate from most problems in life. It's a blessing and a curse.

Regardless of my money situation, making $1000 on a two-minute horse race seemed a thrill worth gambling my last coins away for. It gave me the same dopamine hit that gold does. In a way, prospecting is like gambling—of course, experience and knowledge triumph over sheer luck in prospecting, but the addictive short-term dopamine hits are the same.

I had no idea about the horse number or the jockey, but I gave the $100 to my friend, who was convinced it was going to win—despite not being the favorite. I was just excited that my seventeen-year-old friend, who was not remotely involved in the horse world, evidently had a secret psychic ability to predict race winners! When the horses took off and everyone was cheering at the track, I watched my friend. If he celebrated, I celebrated. I clapped eyes on him just as the horses crossed the finishing line: he was jumping up and down. I had done it! I had won my money back! The feeling was so exhilarating that I bet some of my winnings on more races, but didn't win anything else. I didn't care, though, because my bank account was back up to $900 and I had enough fuel money to move to Melbourne.

Naive is the first word that comes to mind when I remember thinking that amount of money would be anywhere enough. My parents were so supportive that three days before we left, Dad went out prospecting with the intention of giving any gold he found to me for funding the move. Dad found a $3000 nugget that day, and gave me the whole lot.

The horse win and that nugget—a mixture of privilege and the universe having my back—are what enabled me to move to

Melbourne to pursue modeling, and I will always be so thankful. Not only did my parents financially support the move, but they also gave me enough encouragement to program me into believing I would make it. I moved over as a confident, independent, clueless nineteen-year-old and started a new chapter. Saying goodbye to the gold world completely is something I'll never do again, but I am glad nineteen-year-old Tyler had the guts to do it.

Three days after meeting with the agent, the reason we had moved our whole lives to Melbourne, she sent me an email saying they weren't interested. I was lying on a fold-out couch, which we were using as a bed in our thankfully legitimate Melbourne home, when I opened the rejection email. My stomach dropped. I had moved our whole life over to Melbourne because this agency was interested in signing me and after one meeting it was a hard no.

I couldn't believe it. The self-doubt started flowing in—that feeling where your whole body is filled with embarrassment, and you curse your stupidity and doubt your self-worth. All of these emotions were swirling between my stomach and chest, and I started to question why I had ever left my comfortable little box in the first place.

I sat alone in these emotions for a while, too embarrassed to tell anyone, and wondered what I had got so wrong in that interview. When you get rejected from a modeling job, it's someone saying no to your looks, your energy, how photogenic you are, even how you move; it's extremely hard not to take that rejection as a personal attack. I pinpoint this day as the moment I started believing my worth and looks were inherently connected. This mentality is programmed into our brains basically as soon as we leave the womb. A lot of women will wrestle with these beliefs deep down unless they actively work on them, but on that day those beliefs flew into stark consciousness for the first time.

Despite the rejection, I reached out to the five main agencies in Melbourne. They all said no. I thought my modeling career was over. Back then, I didn't have the life experience I have now; I didn't realize there was a reason I didn't get signed with them. I couldn't appreciate that they weren't on the life path that the universe has for me. I couldn't see that getting rejected is just as much a gift as being accepted. Thankfully, even when it didn't seem like everything was happening for a reason, it was.

The house I found on Gumtree in a very dodgy, we-could-get-completely-stuffed-over-here situation was meant to be; Kate, our new neighbor, was good friends with a modeling agent. When she found out that I was trying to pursue modeling, she put us in touch—and within two weeks of those five rejections, I had signed with an agent. My agent then signed me with the modeling agency that I moved to Melbourne for! I was going to be a model. It didn't happen how I had planned, but it did work out. It was a good example of "it's not what you know, but who you know."

In this period of my relationship with Max, I learned very quickly that depression isn't as easy as "toughening up." The days when I would come home to find him lying lifeless on the bed were becoming more frequent; each time I would rush to him wondering if this was the day I would find him dead.

He could never find the words to describe why he was so low. I used to become so frustrated, unable to fathom why he couldn't just tell me what was wrong. I understand now, and if I could turn back time and give him a cuddle instead of an irritable "just tell me," I would—but I can't, and I will always carry that with me.

As time went on and his symptoms worsened, I got better at helping him. My life became dedicated to his happiness. I was happy when he was happy. My emotions and needs came second to his, and I didn't care how I felt as long as he was smiling. I was too young to know how to set boundaries to look after my own mental health. I didn't even recognize what was happening to my wellbeing because I had become such an expert at dissociating. If Max was okay, I was okay.

At this point in our relationship, I had seen him so low that I would excuse almost all of his shitty behavior to keep him feeling okay. I remember he would go missing many times, partying with friends for days on end without contacting me. When I finally got ahold of him, I would be so focused on just making sure his mental health was okay that I wouldn't hold him accountable for his actions.

One day when he had really stuffed up, I went for a walk to clear my mind. I remember thinking to myself, *Wow, this is really hard. How do I know where to draw the line? What do I call him out on and what do I let go?* I wanted to give him a break because he was struggling, but I was also struggling.

I won't say anything this time. I want to be a good girlfriend, I decided. *I will say something next time.*

I never did—well, at least not for a long time. There is a balancing act when supporting a loved one with a mental illness. It's tricky assessing when to let things slide and when to set a boundary.

You can lead a horse to water, but you can't make it drink, as they say, and I learned this watching Max. I didn't understand why he wouldn't get help. I gave him love and support, and the psychologist was free and only a phone call away. It was clear he needed help. He wanted to get better, so why wouldn't he just go?

I took his depression, and reluctance to get help as it worsened, as a personal attack. I couldn't understand why I couldn't fix him. *Is there something wrong with me? He makes me happy, so why can't I make him happy?* None of it made sense. If I could go back to nineteen-year-old Tyler, I would tell her that his mental illness had nothing to do with me. I wasn't there to fix him.

The best thing to do was to support him and give him love— that, and to start looking after my own mental health. Demanding he open up to me only made him feel guilty, which made the situation worse. I wish I'd just given him a hug and told him I didn't appreciate the way he treated me sometimes, and encouraged him to get help without the guilt trip.

I look back and regret some of the things I said and did, but I know they were from a place of love. I was just young and ignorant. I didn't know what depression was, let alone how to support someone through it. Still, I also did a lot of good things that I would appreciate a partner doing for me: I stood by him through numerous job losses; I held him on all the nights he spent feeling low; I researched mental health and educated myself; I never judged the thoughts that he would voice; and I constantly reminded him he was loved, and we would get through it. I did what I could.

I remember one thought he shared that rattled me to my core and made me believe that there was no end in sight. We were visiting his friends and family interstate, and he was just so low. He turned to me and said, "I just don't care. I don't care about anything or anyone."

I asked if he cared about me and he replied that of course he did, but I could tell that he didn't truly mean it. I knew he cared about me in the sense that he loved me and would be upset if I got hurt, but he was clearly quite dead inside.

When you don't care about yourself or what happens to you, you've lost all sense of self. Of course you care about your loved ones, but it's hard to combat that level of apathy. To watch someone hit that degree of depression is heartbreaking. I would rather experience one hell of a depressive episode myself than watch someone I love have to go through it, any day of the week. It's hard on them, it's hard on you; there are no winners. It does teach you new levels of empathy, resilience, and compassion, but it takes a lot of fight to get there.

As the years went by, Max did seek some help and I saw a lot of personal growth in him—but many of the bad habits we formed as seventeen-year-olds stuck around. The issues I let slide when he was struggling became the norm: how we communicated, my lack of boundaries, and the fact his happiness always came before mine. These habits lasted throughout our seven years together, so deeply ingrained that they were impossible to break. Rewiring your brain after struggling with mental illness is so hard, and sometimes triggers never leave—but, though Max's symptoms never fully disappeared, they did improve . . . and as his symptoms started to subside, my own began to arise.

As Max got better and found happiness, I feel like my mind subconsciously started to let down its guard and experience all the emotions that it had spent the past three years dissociating from. It was like I went from not experiencing a single emotion to being trapped in a downhill spiral of anxiety, paranoia, and depression. These were the first serious mental illness symptoms I experienced.

I also began to notice other things: overthinking, racing thoughts, lack of motivation, low energy, tight chest pains, difficulty breathing, and low sex drive. In hindsight, it's clear I was experiencing depression and anxiety, but at the time I was convinced that I just didn't know how to properly deal with life stressors. I was convinced that all adults felt that way, and I just wasn't handling it properly.

I had just moved out of home and started a new job, so I thought it was normal for those things to cause stress and assumed I just wasn't coping. This denial was one of the reasons I refused help. I was not very good at communicating that I was struggling, but my actions and temperament made it clear something wasn't quite right.

I was moody, irritable, and miserable. I was good at hiding those negative symptoms from people around me, because I subconsciously knew the person I had become wasn't great to be around. The only person I found it too hard to keep up the act around was Max. He copped the bad Tyler, and as the years went on, more of my nearest and dearest got to meet her too.

The next two years in Melbourne were a whirlwind. In addition to a bit of modeling and running my jewelry business, I was deep in the world of hospitality, working at the bar College Lawn as a functions and events manager. It was the best two years of my life. I started as a bartender and within six months started to work my way up the management ladder.

It was fast-paced and intense, and the venue became my life. I was working just off Chapel Street and became best friends with the other bartenders there. A lot of them were backpackers who loved to party; Chapel Street nightlife was insane. Claire, Indi, Cienna, and my other friends were, and still are, the best support network. I loved the food, the drinks, and the partying. At some points, I loved it all a little too much.

Although I adored working in the bar and Melbourne life, another side of me was really struggling. It was like I was living a double life. I look back now and realize that while I loved Melbourne, it wasn't me. It buried a part of my soul and made me feel lost.

Money was a big source of stress and I am lucky I had my parents. I can't remember how many times I called them, crying for rent money—I truly can't imagine how I would have got through without that privilege. It was easy to blame money struggles for my bad mood, easy to think that I would be happy if I just had a little more money. Again, naive. It's hard to explain to someone what mental illness feels like if they haven't experienced it; it's not something that is easy to comprehend. Even now, six years into this journey, on my good days I struggle to remember exactly how the bad days felt. I am quickly reminded when they come back around, though.

One day, I was driving home after finishing a long shift behind the bar when I spotted a family laughing in the park. It was nothing out of the ordinary, but that moment hit me. I had really forgotten what happiness felt like. I sat there and tried to remember the last time I'd felt happy, and I really couldn't.

The first depressive symptoms I started to experience were much more physical than mental. I was totally lethargic and my sleeping patterns were a mess. Disturbed sleeping patterns are a key symptom of mental health issues, and it's still one of my main indicators that something is going on for me. I was sleeping twelve hours a night, but would be so lethargic by 3 p.m. that I would be unable to get off my bedroom floor. It was such a different feeling from usual tiredness—it's not how you feel after a big day at the beach or a shitty night's sleep. It felt like my bones were lead.

During the day I would lie on the bedroom floor for hours, unable to move, like I was paralyzed. My mind would tell me I was lazy, but my heavy bones couldn't climb off the floor. Depression is strange; it lies and tricks you. If I was out with friends, the feeling would disappear for just enough time to fool me into thinking I was fine—maybe even that I was making it up.

In the mornings before work, I would sit on the couch for three hours watching TV and it would be the same feeling. It made me feel so guilty, but I really couldn't help it. My motivation was nonexistent, but I never acknowledged it. I tricked myself into thinking my nonexistent motivation was a sign of laziness and I just needed to learn how to structure my day better, or learn how to get up to my alarm, or start journaling instead of sitting on my phone. I thought I was useless when I was sick.

I ended up taking myself to my GP because I was convinced I had anaemia. I had struggled with it in the past, and to me that was the only explanation for why I was feeling so flat. My GP ran some tests and they came back fine: my iron levels and everything else were perfect. I was gobsmacked.

I asked her to run more tests because I was certain an iron deficiency was the only explanation. The next sentence to come out of her mouth was a pivotal moment in my life. It set off a butterfly effect.

"Tyler, your bloods are fine, but how is your mental health?" she asked.

It was the first time in my life I had ever been asked that question, and every emotion I'd been avoiding flooded straight into my brain. My throat dried up, my stomach sank, and I started crying. It was like my mind had been begging me to pay attention to it—and for the first time in years, I was forced to.

9

MIND SHAFTS

I don't know what it is about human nature and our need to answer "How are you?" with "Yeah, I'm fine," no matter what. Is it to save face? To not burden people? To appear brave? Is vulnerability too scary? It's always my first response, and I think there is a mixture of reasons for that. Admitting I wasn't fine would mean admitting that I needed help—and that would mean facing my own demons when it felt much easier to ignore them.

Another reason I find it difficult to truthfully answer "how are you" is that as much as people want to help others, it's tricky knowing what to do when someone does admit they aren't okay. We aren't taught in school how to respond to that. I have learned over time that just speaking about your issues lightens the mental load, but for a long time I kept quiet. I believed that the demons were so at home in my mind that no amount of sharing would shake them, that no one else could help—so why waste my breath?

When my GP asked about my mental health, I said, "Well, I have been a little anxious lately, maybe." I couldn't understand my mental health and what was happening at all, let alone explain it to someone else. Fortunately, this answer was enough for her to recommend me to a psychologist and not just throw some anxiety medication at me.

Medication has its place in mental illness recovery, but if my GP had just tried to fix me with medicine instead of enlisting the help of a psych to get to the root of my problems, who knows what would have happened. Medication can make symptoms worse if they are used or administered incorrectly, something else I later learned the hard way.

After my GP referred me to a psychologist, it took me months to make the appointment. I could not be bothered opening the vault and unleashing all the thoughts I had spent years suppressing. I had enough going on; Max and I were fending for ourselves in Melbourne. We were broke, and I was working a job with a fair bit of responsibility for a twenty-year-old. I thought to myself, *It's all situational. It will pass.*

It didn't.

I finally made the appointment to see a psychologist; with the referral from my GP, I received ten subsidized sessions. I know for a fact if I'd had to pay for that appointment, I would not have gone. This is something else I am so grateful for—it's so much harder for people living in places that don't have this luxury. People often commend me on how I've handled my mental health journey, but I am honestly just a product of my privilege. Without Medicare, a supportive family, my education, the ability to critically think, and much more, my story would have already ended.

The only person who knew I was going to that appointment was

Max. I had so many supportive people in my life I could have leaned on, but in my mind, it was easier to fight it alone. I knew I would be fine eventually, so why would I stress out my loved ones? I wish I could tell my twenty-year-old self that even though she could fight it alone, she didn't have to. People need people, and there is nothing wrong with that. Love and support don't take away the darkness, but instead hold your hand and shine a light.

When I walked into the psychologist's office, I sat down and cried and cried and cried. I was so embarrassed I had spent five minutes crying that I could barely look her in the eyes. She diagnosed me with depression and minor anxiety. I saw her twice and then stopped; she was a good psychologist and I liked her, but I just couldn't be bothered. I had dissociating from problems down pat, and hoped that if I ignored them, they would go away. I'm slowly learning that isn't the case.

A year went by, and my symptoms got progressively worse—especially the anxiety. It took over my life and slowly transformed into paranoia. It started off as the sort of feeling where you know for a fact everyone in your PE class is talking about you. Then it became pressing: you might get home from work and stay awake until the opening shift, staring at your phone because you're adamant you made a mistake and someone is going to message you to tell you off. After this, it started to escalate into the type of paranoia that makes it hard to function.

One night, around 2 a.m., I locked up the pub after work and drove home. On the way, I was waiting at a red light when the guy parked next to me made eye contact with me. My mind went into panic, convinced he was loading a gun. He was fiddling with something on his lap and looking at me. I knew deep in my heart he was loading a gun to kill me. My stomach sank and I assessed that I either had to run the red light or sit there waiting for him to shoot me. I ran the red light and took the long way home, looking over my shoulder at every turn and contemplating calling the police. My fifteen-minute car ride turned into a thirty-minute panic attack. I got home and went straight to bed, wired from my near-death experience.

A month or so later, I ended up coming out of that paranoid haze and realized that he had just been on his phone or rolling a cigarette. He was probably only staring at me because I was staring at *him,* like a deer in headlights.

I told Max, "I think I overexaggerated that story and no one was trying to shoot me." He replied that he knew that, but didn't want to make me mad, so he kept quiet.

A few weeks later, I was walking my dog to the local store and a woman was walking just behind me. I noticed she started taking every single turn I did. Was she following me? I started to walk more quickly and so did she. She was probably trying to grab me—I had seen a white van earlier. I told myself to keep calm and just pick up the pace, but then she did as well. She was following me, no question. I had to escape. I put down my shopping bags and ran for it.

I was running as fast as I could through the suburbs of Melbourne and calling Max to come and save me. I couldn't go home—the van was probably watching and waiting to see where I would go. I found the nearest park and hid in some trees until Max arrived, scooping me up and saving me from a human trafficking scheme.

Soon after that episode, I again realized that the woman

was probably just walking to the shops too. How could I believe something to be so true, so real, only to realize weeks later just how crazy it was?

I started to question every one of my thoughts, and reality started to become a little hard for me to grasp. At this point it became obvious to me that I needed help—and yet I still refused it. My decision-making skills were very poor, and at a time when I should have been nurturing my physical and mental health, I decided to actively destroy both.

I started partying heavily—maybe not heavily for some, but enough to really impact my life. It's strange because although I had this darkness in me that was set on self-destruction, I still had an angelic voice in my mind telling me to be better, work hard, stay fit, and succeed. That "good" Tyler, dedicated to self-improvement and success, became obsessed.

It was a different sort of self-destruction. Not the "party and drugs" type, but destruction disguised as personal growth. Like a wolf in sheep's clothing, it may have seemed good on a superficial level, but deep down that mindset was doing me serious harm.

The habits I cultivated—healthy eating, exercise, and working hard—were great on paper, but I took them all to extremes and used them as another means to hurt myself. I never realized at the time. People tried to tell me, but it wasn't until after years of self-reflecting, looking at photos, and unlearning bad habits that I could look back and realize how much damage I was doing to myself.

Body image and disordered eating began to control my life. I never noticed it as an issue at the time, and it has now taken me five years of rewiring my brain to break down my problems from that period in my life. The damage I did in this time has been some of the most permanent. Not a day goes by that I don't have to manage my disordered eating patterns, and I know this is probably a fight I will have to face forever.

I am better now at hearing those voices in my head, recognizing that they are toxic, and telling them to be quiet. Sometimes, though, the conversation takes a while. I'll stand at the fridge for ten to fifteen minutes, convincing myself that even though I have already eaten three times that day, I am allowed to have a meal after netball training. Eventually, I can silence the little voice telling me to close the fridge door. These patterns are not all my fault—in fact, they are mostly the patriarchy's—but it is still my responsibility to resist them so I can enjoy my life and not fear passing them onto my children or the women around me.

Even from infancy, we learn that our worth is tied to our weight and what we look like. Western beauty standards are relentless, and that's coming from someone who generally fits them! Twenty-year-old Tyler was brainwashed to believe she needed to be a size 6 to feel any sort of self-worth. This feeling stemmed from what I saw out in the world and on social media, particularly when I began modeling. The idea of gaining weight sent shivers down my spine, so I did everything in my power to make sure I always fitted my size 6 jeans. I truly believed that I mattered because I was skinny. It became a personality trait. Being in the modeling industry didn't help the situation, even though I thought I was better than that. I always said that the 'you're too big' comments or 'your measurements are huge' digs didn't impact me.

I insisted I didn't care if I missed out on a job because of my size, but now I realize it was probably impacting me so much more than I gave it credit for. At one casting for David Jones there was a girl with scars on her wrists sitting next to me, and I remember thinking I was glad that I was too strong and tough for rejection to hurt me. I even told my mum that it was so lucky I wasn't like that girl, and could handle the industry.

I started self-harming two years later.

Money was a big source of stress for Max and me, as it is for most young people. I would always have so much anxiety around money and how I wasn't saving anything. Of course, for all those times I didn't save money in Melbourne, I gained moments money can't buy—precious memories.

I have never regretted my financial choices at that point in my life, whether it was choosing a weekend on the coast, or a night out at a cocktail bar or fancy restaurant, instead of having a night in and saving my money. I will have those experiences forever; I truly lived my life during that time. There is a point in your life when you need to grow up, and I am glad I didn't choose when I was in my early twenties in Melbourne to do so.

Now that I am older and starting to settle a little more, it is such a relief for me to look back on these years and remember all those amazing experiences and moments. In life you will always have to make sacrifices. I sacrificed saving money, buying a home, having kids young, and investing my money. Sometimes it gets me down and I feel like I have wasted so much time, but you can't have it all.

Those sacrifices meant I got countless nights out with friends, moved across the country, started a business at twenty, enjoyed so many amazing things, and made many meaningful connections that I will have forever. Living my life, creating memories, and taking risks mean more to me than playing it safe.

The first customer for my jewelry business was Hannah, one of my best friends at College Lawn. She bought a stardust ring and started a craze at work. Everyone wanted one; that ring alone funded my business cards and my first collection photoshoot, even leaving me with enough money to reinvest in a second collection.

I would bring a shoebox full of my handmade jewelry into work and everyone would pick out what they wanted. I would never have been able to start my business, let alone keep it running, if it wasn't for my friends. The support they gave me was truly life-changing; not only did they keep Mae by Tyler afloat throughout its four years, but they also believed in me when I couldn't believe in myself. On the slow sale days, a random order from my best friend Sarah would come in and reassure me that my business wasn't shit. Every single month, even as the business grew bigger and bigger, my friends were putting through a large number of the orders. I will never be able to repay them for what they have done for my entrepreneurial journey, but I know if they hadn't been backing me at every turn, I would have given up years ago.

As my little jewelry business started to grow, I realized the thing I really needed in my career was to be my own boss. I liked doing things when I wanted and how I wanted. I was a manager at the bar by the time I was twenty-one, but every day I still manifested that I would be able to leave and fully pursue my own business venture.

I was still employed as a casual, and I loved it because every week looked different. My venue manager wanted to make me full time, but it felt claustrophobic to me. Sure, the sick days and paid leave would have been great for my bank account, but the idea of it made me feel stuck and I didn't like that. Casual employment also worked for me because I often swapped shifts when modeling gigs popped up; as much as I loved that bar and being part of events there, I couldn't bring myself to fully commit to it. I always kept space for my business and modeling.

My jewelry began to gain some traction when Steph Claire Smith, who is arguably Australia's biggest Instagram influencer, wore a pair of my earrings. I had 200 orders overnight. My jewelry was all handmade, and those earrings took thirty minutes each to make. I moved my tiny bench from our lounge room to a proper office space in our spare room. My goal was to eventually have a proper office that isn't in my home, and this was a good start. My office has slowly progressed over the years since then, but it's nice to look back on what it was.

My business model was quite old school. All of those orders had to be individually created and sent, and the money was paid via bank transfer, which added hours and hours to my admin. My parents were very old school in the way they operated their shop, so it was just what felt normal to me—but I knew my life would be a million times easier if I had a website.

I had a small amount of money in my Mae by Tyler account at this point and I was reinvesting everything I earned back into the business—more stock, cameras, and marketing. There was about $1000 in the account when I wanted to make the website. It was back in 2015—before Squarespace, Shopify, Wix, and the like had come onto the scene—so I decided to hire someone to make it for me. I first went to one of the security guard's sons at work, having been told he was an expert. He was not.

I gave him $300 to build the website and after six months he hadn't even made the home page. When I went around to his house once for a "design" meeting, it was pitch black inside and his mum was lying on a couch in the lounge room, smoking weed. He took me to his back room, and we sat at his gaming desk. I wondered how I'd ended up in a weed-filled two-bedroom apartment in St. Kilda trying to get a website out of my local security guard's son. *How did I get here and how do I get out?* I asked for a refund and after another two months his dad handed me $150 cash at work, and that was the end of that. It was onto plan B, and at that point I thought my lesson was that you get what you pay for.

I decided that if I was going to make this website, I was going to do it properly. I googled away, found a website-building company in Melbourne, and organized a meeting. I put on my best business outfit and marched my twenty-one-year-old arse and $1000 down to their city office. Naivety seems to be a theme of my younger twenties, but I guess that's what those years are for. Even though I look back at that day and can't help but think about how I was about to be completely ripped off and begin years of credit card debt, it really was one of those rare moments of feeling successful. It's a feeling I've really struggled with over my life, and it wasn't until much later that I allowed myself to conceive of success as not being tied to wealth. There are a handful of little moments in my life that made me feel a wave of "I'm doing it" or "I've done it"—little sparks of pride—and this was one of them.

I sat around a table with four people in suits and discussed what I wanted. They quoted me $11,000 for a website, which included design, hosting, and SEO for an extra cost, plus three months of free changes and then some support after. I was a little bit taken aback by the quote, but I didn't let on that I thought it was a lot of money. I played it cool and said I would get back to them by the end of the week. Something my bar job taught me is to never show your fears or anxieties. Instead I say, "Yep, I've got this," and then figure it out later. I needed a website. I had been stuffed around for months and I had no idea how to build one alone, so no matter what anyone said, I was going to do it.

I convinced myself it was a good idea. I'm pretty good at that—combine that skill with impulsivity and there wasn't much chance of twenty-one-year-old me saying no to that offer. I rang Mum and Dad, who told me it was my business and they would support what I wanted to do. Within the week, I'd signed an $11,000 contract with $1000 in my business account. It is cringe-worthy to think about, but this was an "oh well" moment. Although it was poorly considered and very risky, I do pat baby Tyler on the back for her extreme self-confidence. I signed that contract because I backed myself. I knew I would make it work—there was zero space in my head for it not working, and not once did I think I wouldn't pull it off. I like to think my brain is a mixture of confidence, bravery, and delusion.

I had a payment plan where I had $2000 due every month for six months. I had the first month covered with personal savings (which only had $1000 in it) and the business's savings. I was certain I would figure out how to get the money every month. The website would be finished in three months, and after that I thought website sales would cover it. By that reckoning, I only had to worry about the next two payments.

I quickly realized, though, that my sales were not enough to cover the repayments, so I decided to get a credit card. Westpac and ANZ both gave me one with a $3000 limit each, so I had over half the website paid for. The $6000 credit card debt never made me stressed—anytime an anxious thought about it came into my head I would remind myself that it was only $6000 and I would eventually pay it back. Samantha Wills, who is an incredible Australian entrepreneur and jewelry designer, was $60,000 in debt at my age; I figured if she could do it then so could I.

Time went by and the rest of the payment was due. Max and I were super tight on money and living paycheck to paycheck. It was extremely hard and a massive strain on our relationship. I still needed more money for the website, but I couldn't get any more credit cards in my name—so Mum gave me one of her credit cards and Max took one out in his name. I split the remaining payments between the two of them. Another example of how privileged I was in the early years of my business: my family backed me enough to financially support me. Not only did the money help, but them trusting me like that gave me so much confidence.

After taking credit card interest rates into account, I ended up spending $12,000 on that website, plus an annual fee of $840. I only kept the website for three years before moving to a better hosting platform, but it put me in debt for much longer. It took me four years to pay everything off, which hurt my financials for a long time—but not that long, in the scheme of things.

Every time I go to make an impulsive decision, I think of the lessons that website saga taught me. When asked what my biggest regret in life is, that website springs to mind. While it taught me a great lesson, it's one I could have learned without spending so much money—but I think it needed to happen. Now, I build my websites at a monthly cost of $40.

In any case, the jewelry business grew. Not only were we stocked in Australian stores, but we also gained some international customers. Running an ecommerce store was like gold prospecting for me: you wake up in the morning and have no idea how much you will make. There is always the glittering thought that tomorrow could be the day. I loved it.

Even though I had tried to escape the gold game, I never truly did. Sure, I wasn't living in the outback digging for gold every day, but I was always chasing those same highs and the same lifestyle.

One day I got an exciting email that my favorite swimwear designer, who is a huge name in the Australian swimming world, was opening a store in Sydney—and they wanted to stock my jewelry. I could not believe it.

Imposter syndrome tried to strike, but I pushed it aside and reminded myself that I could do this. I spent three days handmaking enough jewelry to stock the store, popped it in a box, and sent it to Sydney by post, just in time for the opening. Everything was good, until I got a phone call in the middle of work. My package had gone missing. All those pieces were gone, and it was the day before open day.

I was devastated. Not only had $2000 worth of my stock gone missing, but I had also let down this big brand. I've said before that

I walk through every door that is opened for me and figure out the rest later—this was the time to figure out the rest. I called the brand and said I would be there in the morning, with product, in time for the 11 a.m. launch.

So as any sane twenty-one-year-old would do on a Thursday at 5 p.m., I swapped my shift at work for the next day, booked an 8 a.m. flight to Sydney, and stayed up until 3 a.m. making another whole collection.

I flew into Sydney, dropped it off, caught up with a friend, and went home to Melbourne that night. Everything worked out in the end. Despite that little shitstorm in the middle, everything was where it was meant to be. I also ended up getting back the original box—thank you, Australia Post, for the complete fuck-around.

10

DRY PANNING BACK WEST

Reflecting on those days I spent working behind a bar and aiming to scale the management ladder is interesting. As I've grown, I have begun to understand my own actions and thought patterns more clearly, as well as how the patriarchy impacts all aspects of life.

When I was twenty years old and working as a casual bartender, I was trying to prove I'd be a good fit for the next duty manager role. A girl around my age had begun working there as a casual as well; she was a legend and we got along like a house on fire. She had around my level of experience and knowledge in hospitality; I would say our initiative, creativity, leadership qualities, bartending skills, people skills, time management, and common sense were all about the same. She hadn't even expressed an interest in becoming a manager, but in my mind, she became an instant threat.

The interesting part is that there were a couple of guys on our level who could also have been promoted to duty manager, but I was never threatened by them. Even though we were theoretically equals,

I thought I would have to wait for them to be promoted first—and then it would be a fight between the other girl and me.

This wasn't a hurdle that my workplace had created; I had an amazing boss who would never consciously favor men. He always gave me just as many opportunities as he gave any of my male colleagues. It was a very deeply rooted belief that I had constructed in my mind, and formed from growing up and working in such a male-dominated field.

My whole life I saw hardly any women succeeding and climbing the ranks. I grew up to believe that there were fewer job opportunities for women, which meant when there was another woman, she was direct competition. There were never two female managers, I believed. It had to be either you or me; there wasn't room for both. It has taken me years to realize there is room—we just have to make it.

There are invisible hurdles women face in the workplace that can't be noted as a statistic. They seem like minor setbacks but are part of why women must work twice as hard to get to the same place as men. The privilege of being a cis-hetero man living under the patriarchy doesn't necessarily mean a life of luxury and smooth sailing. It's not extra points; it's the absence of extra penalties. When we speak on these issues, the only way we can move forward is for the people benefiting from patriarchal structures (namely, cis-hetero men) to listen to and believe us . . . but how can we overcome the extra hurdles when many men don't even see them?

After two years of living in Melbourne, I had been out of the gold game for a while and I had my mind set on becoming an entrepreneur—until I got a call from my parents asking if I wanted to join them on a TV show about gold prospecting.

Mum and Dad were asked to be on the show *Aussie Gold Hunters* via a contact from the gold shop. They'd originally said no—my parents are very private people who keep to themselves—but the paycheck was simply too good to turn down. After some convincing, I said I would fly back to Perth in the middle of summer, leaving my hospitality job right in peak time.

That was *very* hard to do—if you know, you know. If it wasn't for my amazing venue manager letting me take time off then, I would never have got to where I am today. That little bit of understanding gave me the start to a career in TV. I didn't think like this at the time, though; I just thought of it as some quick money, nothing long-term. Little did I know, *Aussie Gold Hunters* would become one of the most popular TV shows on Discovery Channel and lead me to a gig on *Gold Rush*.

I went back home to Kalgoorlie for filming, and loved it. It truly made me realize how much I had missed the red dirt, the gold, and the community. One thing I really struggled with living in Melbourne was the lack of community. Of course, big towns have pockets of tight-knit communities too, but anyone from the country will tell you it is not the same. Being from a country community gives you a sense of belonging and safety you don't get in the city. I realized I really missed that and that being away from the goldfields had hugely impacted my mental health. While I was there, Mum and I were walking and laughing on a salt lake in Kalgoorlie when I had a flashback to my first week working at the bar. I'd served some guy and when I gave him his beer he said, "You're from the country, aren't you?" When I replied yes, he said, "You can just tell. Never lose that; it's special."

I didn't understand what he meant at the time, but in that moment with Mum it finally clicked. I had lost that. I wanted that back. I knew exactly what he meant, and I felt like crap realizing it was gone.

Melbourne had taken a huge toll on my mental health. I was struggling fiercely with body dysmorphia and disordered eating to the point that I couldn't eat a meal without it being an issue. I think my disordered eating emerged from a perfect storm—being away from gold, living so far from my family, toxic traits in my relationship, money, and self-worth issues, my predisposition to mental illness, and imposter syndrome.

My modeling agency was of course a big part of this; they put huge pressure on me to be thin. Even though they liked to say they supported healthy models, it was all bullshit. They wanted you as thin as your bones would let you be. When I was at my worst, I couldn't even eat an Oreo without crying. The agency sent me a Christmas card that said: "Congratulations on your new body, Tyler!" Pretty disgusting, hey?

I was completely delusional about my body. Diet and exercise were ruling my life and had a chokehold on my brain. I was working out nine times a week and eating extremely "cleanly." I could not go half a day without obsessing over my diet and exercise regime, or without finding a mirror to check that I still had abs. If you had told that Tyler that in five years' time, she would have no abs and be over 20 pounds heavier (but a whole lot happier) I honestly think she would have had a psychotic break. The thought of gaining weight truly terrified me. I was out for dinner once and when my salad was served with dressing, I couldn't eat it; the thought of consuming that dressing made my heart want to stop beating. Even chocolate powder on a cappuccino was enough to send me into tears.

In those times I missed out on so many amazing moments with people I cherish. I try to remind myself that I am not to blame. We live in a society where counting calories is praised as healthy, eating cheese and biscuits is called a cheat meal, and having a glass of wine with your partner means you need to go for a run.

Companies that profit off insecurity label food as good and bad, and these messages seeped into my brain. They extol the virtues of super foods and workout plans that you *need* if you want to look like this amazing influencer—but let's conveniently leave out that her thigh gap is the result of genetics. If these same companies allocated time, effort, and money to teaching young people that food is fuel, not something that is inherently good or bad, and that exercising is just as good for the mind as it is for the body, maybe we wouldn't have a generation of girls who fear vinaigrette.

I still fight these thoughts every day and must regularly convince myself that I am still amazing even if my jeans don't fit. The turning point for me happened at the same time as we were filming *Aussie Gold Hunters*. I was at a Kalgoorlie pub with an old friend and ordered an espresso martini—only with no sugar syrup and no Kahlúa, so just a glass of coffee and vodka. It was a usual order for me. My friend asked why I did that, and I explained that the sugar in the drink would make me gain weight.

I will never forget the look on her face. She replied, "Who told you that?"

I was a bit taken aback. All I could say was, "Well, you know, sugar makes you fat."

She gave me a big hug and said, "Tyler, having a drink that actually tastes good with me won't make you fat—and even if it did, that is very fatphobic. You're better than that."

It was the slap in the face I needed. The next day I ate a whole pack of crackers, and amazingly the world did not end.

After a year of actively denying my depression diagnosis in hopes that it would disappear, the panic attacks became worse and more frequent. I just accepted that it was a part of life, and became a professional at making it seem like I was fine to the outside world.

I was partying heavily, spending money like crazy, doing recreational drugs, and staying out until 6 a.m. when I had to start work at 10 a.m. I was making stupid decisions that were not a reflection of my values at all. I was irritated, irrational, and reckless. In hindsight, I was experiencing my first manic episode.

My second manic episode, which I would experience a little later in life, was a lot more serious. Still, I wish I'd picked up on my bipolar symptoms right then and there, because unfortunately I got worse. My mental health started to greatly impact my relationship and Max set a very fair boundary, saying that if I didn't get help, he would leave me.

I didn't take him seriously; I was still living in denial. I didn't want to tell anyone about it because I was terrified that I was making up my mental health problems for attention, so I reasoned that this couldn't be true if I kept my mouth shut.

At this point we decided to move from Melbourne back to Perth. There were a few reasons, but at the end of the day we just felt like it was time. I wanted to be closer to my family, and I wanted back into the gold world, even if I wasn't ready to fully commit to it again quite yet. Instead, when we moved to Perth I began working at bars again and concentrating on Mae by Tyler. I was determined for my business to work, and I think this is the reason I didn't move straight back to Kalgoorlie with my family and commit to gold. I was still set on owning and running Mae by Tyler full-time, and I had to work at the bar to support that.

Besides, moving back to Kalgoorlie would have felt like a step back. I know now how silly that is, but at the time I thought if I moved to Perth and worked on Mae by Tyler, I wasn't a failure for leaving Melbourne. So, Perth it was: close enough to the Goldfields and my family, but far enough away for me to think I hadn't failed.

It was very hard for me to leave my functions manager role at College Lawn. I had been there from the very start of my Melbourne adventure, and we were a family. My boss, Mark, and other colleagues had helped me so much over those two and a half years. I had grown so much and if it wasn't for Mark and that job, I would not be who I am today. I made friends who will be part of my life forever. Without that job and those friends, I would have hated Melbourne and I wouldn't have launched Mae by Tyler; they supported it from the start. It was a big chapter in my life I now had to put to rest.

Before I left Melbourne, I was at work one day when I decided to leave the bar to go check the schedule. Because I did that, I overheard a conversation between two work friends. My friend Grace was explaining that she had been feeling anxious, so she had booked in with a psychologist. The psychologist had diagnosed Grace with anxiety; she had started therapy, and was feeling better already.

Hearing about someone else actively dealing with their shit made me want to do the same. I didn't want to live in denial anymore, and she gave me hope that I could heal my mind. It was such a simple conversation, but it shifted my perspective. Just when things were getting bad, the universe had my back. I was in the right place at the right time.

For the first time, I seriously wanted to try and fix my declining mental health, which didn't improve much even once I was back in Perth. I had seen a psychologist before in Melbourne, but didn't really click with him, which made it hard. It didn't help that throughout the time I was seeing him, I was going in and out of episodes—which meant sometimes I went to my appointment and sometimes I just ghosted him. When I booked in with a new psychologist in Perth, I was determined to do better, but that didn't always happen.

I can't even count how many times I would feel elated, decide that I was "fixed," and skip therapy—only for it all to come crashing down again. I would feel like I was trapped in a dark hole with no lights and no way out—a deep, empty feeling that I would swear black and blue would last forever. Then, I would come out of that episode and not be able to relate to that Tyler at all. I would look back and call myself crazy because I was fine and didn't recognize this depressed person, all in the space of a few months. It was crazy how I could feel so horrifically low and then come out of it. I would write notes in my phone about how horrible I felt, only to read them a week later and be genuinely confused about how I could have written them.

During my elated periods, I would be reckless with no understanding of consequences. For about four months, I would drive to work in Perth and park as close as I could because I was always running late. That meant I was always parking illegally, and a couple of times a week I would get a $70 parking fine. I would grab the fine, shove it in my glove box, and never think about it again. I could totally dissociate from it, and just couldn't fathom that eventually there would be a consequence.

One day, Max found them all shoved in there and became infuriated. I can now see why he would be: there were thousands of dollars of unpaid fines; we shared a bank account at the time, so it impacted him too. I could not see that, though, and honestly just wanted him to fuck off and mind his own business. I ended up coming out of that haze owing $3000 worth of parking tickets. I put it on my credit card. Apparently, consequences do catch up to you.

After months of this, my Perth psychologist finally concluded that he thought I had bipolar disorder. I still remember the words coming out of his mouth. At first it was a weight off my shoulders because I had an excuse for acting like a maniac, literally. The doubt quickly hit me, though—had I made all of this up? Had I answered the questions perfectly to ensure that was the diagnosis? Was I searching for an excuse to make stupid decisions? I still didn't really understand bipolar at the time; I thought it meant I had two personalities.

Psychologists in Australia cannot officially diagnose bipolar or administer any medication, so he referred me to a psychiatrist for a second opinion and hopefully a diagnosis. I rang Max and told him the news; he was the only person I told for a long time. His reaction was what I expected: he was confused and asked if I was sure. I just said that I didn't know either.

I put off seeing the psychiatrist for a little while, but eventually I bit the bullet and made the appointment. I was a nervous wreck driving there; I wanted to keep living my life like everything was fine and there wasn't an issue. It was so much easier than facing the fact I was mentally unwell.

I walked into the office with my eyes glued to the ground. I could barely look the receptionist in the eyes. I just felt so embarrassed. I walked into the psychiatrist's office and all I could think of saying to her was "I am fine"—but for the first time ever, that response wasn't enough. I had to face what was going on in my own mind. I cried for the first five minutes, even though I was trying to do anything and everything to avoid the tears. I have since learned it's easier to let them fall.

She asked me a series of questions and I filled out multiple in-depth questionnaires. At the end of the session she officially diagnosed me with Type 1 Bipolar. Finally. It was 2018—a long five years after this mental illness had started taking over my life. It was a pivotal milestone. Unfortunately, I was still fighting a lot of denial at the time; it would be another two years before I took that diagnosis seriously. I wish I could go back and tell that Tyler to take that psychiatrist's conclusion to heart. I would tell her that she was sick, but it was beatable if she worked hard at it. Instead, over the next couple of years, my mental health continued to get a lot worse before it got better.

The treatment plan was medication and fortnightly sessions with an in-house psychologist who worked in the same clinic as my psychiatrist, which was very helpful because they could communicate as needed. Those sessions helped a lot. We were targeting my depression and anxiety at this stage because they were impacting my life the most, and we did a lot of schema therapy. Schemas are core themes that repeat throughout our lives, and eventually become core beliefs. We can react in a couple of ways to these: some people surrender to their schemas; some find ways to block them out; others fight back and overcompensate in the process.

The major schema I struggled with and completely surrendered to was approval seeking. Having this schema meant I had a deep belief that I was not worthy unless I was gaining recognition or attention from other people—which came at the expense of developing a secure, genuine sense of self. My self-esteem was dependent on others. This led to me making big life decisions that were not true reflections of what I wanted for myself. I also struggled with a hypersensitivity to rejection.

Once I was aware this was going on, I was able to change the narrative in my mind. Understanding those schemas nurtured my self-awareness, which has been a blessing and a curse. It's given me the ability to reflect on my paranoia and be more aware of where my mental state is at, and how it's affecting my relationships and the people around me. On the other hand, it's been extremely painful knowing my thoughts sometimes make zero sense, but having no ability to stop or resist them.

One day, my best friend was being a little quiet at drinks, and I had convinced myself that it was because she hated me. Before schema therapy, I probably would have asked repeatedly if she was mad or if I had said something to upset her. There really was nothing wrong; she was just tired. Instead of asking her repeatedly if she was mad at me, I just self-reflected. After a few sessions of schema therapy, I could stop those thoughts in their tracks and remind myself that it was my schema talking, not the truth. I could observe my thoughts instead of being completely consumed by them, and that was really life-changing for me.

The second half of my treatment was medication, which was just as important as the therapy. The first lot I was placed on made my blood pressure drop so much that I fainted. I went back to the psychiatrist, and she prescribed lithium instead. Lithium is the standard for bipolar treatment and acts as a mood stabilizer, tremendously leveling out the extreme highs and lows if it is taken correctly.

When the psychiatrist read out the side effects of lithium and I heard the words "weight gain," I froze. I could not fathom gaining weight—it was the worst-case scenario in my mind—so I pushed back on starting lithium. I genuinely put fitting into a size 6 pair of jeans above the treatment of a serious mental illness that was slowly devastating my life.

My fear of weight gain mixed with diagnosis denial led me to take my lithium very sporadically. I have since learned that this is the worst thing you can do. Go figure. Taking lithium irregularly actually magnifies bipolar symptoms—so much so that it would have been better to just not take it at all.

I think this was one of the reasons I started experiencing a mixed state, which is when you experience depressive and manic symptoms simultaneously. It's hard to explain, but for me it was the emptiness and loneliness of depression coexisting with the recklessness and impulsiveness of mania. For me, it was being suicidal and having the ability to act on it.

It was terrifying.

11

THE PROSPECTORS CLUB

In many ways, living back in Western Australia was great for my mental health, but I still had to deal with my worst enemy: myself. Not only was I fighting demons in my own head, but a big part of me also didn't want to admit they were there, regardless of my diagnosis.

Fortunately (or unfortunately) I had a lot to keep me distracted. I was working as a functions and events manager at a bar called The Aviary Perth while running Mae by Tyler, and in summer I filmed for *Aussie Gold Hunters*. I had grown up a little bit; I was twenty-three, and there was a lot more life experience under my belt. I was closer to the goldfields, my family, and my community, and I would often head back home to prospect with the family. My top priority at the time was still Mae by Tyler—not necessarily the jewelry itself, but "making it" as an entrepreneur.

Looking back, I was experiencing a high degree of hypermania. Max was working an hour and a half away and only came home on weekends, so I would have to squeeze in trips to see him during the week. Add to that: thirty-five hours a week working at the bar and its sister bar; playing state league netball, which required me to train three times a week; running my jewelry business; starting a vegan catering company; running a vegan events company; and fostering dogs on the side. Then, I launched a sustainable swimwear line—because why not?

My parents were always extremely supportive of me, but my jam-packed schedule was veering toward unhealthy at this point. What I was doing wasn't smart. They suggested I stick to one thing and make that thing great, but my hypermanic brain insisted on doing everything all at once. When I am in that headspace it's go-go-go, and slowing down makes me feel like a failure. I thought the busier I was, the more successful I was—a toxic state of mind that living in a capitalist society reinforces. I had yet to learn that I'm worth more than the hours I worked per week, and that rest is not for the lazy.

When I started the sustainable swimwear business, I had zero idea about fashion—no clue about patternmaking, design, sourcing, or sampling. I didn't even have a retail background, but I woke up one day and decided I wanted to make swimwear, so I did. I found lycra that was made from 100 percent recycled plastic, which was collected in the Mediterranean Sea and repurposed for textiles in Italy. It was beautiful fabric, and I was very proud to use it. The first time I met with the sales rep, I took a notebook. I didn't let on that I was a rookie—I winged it the whole way—and by the end of our meeting, the notebook was filled with phrases to google, because I did not understand a word she was saying.

Next, I needed to find a manufacturer, but I couldn't find one whose sustainability practices and ethics I was happy with, and who also had a low enough minimum order quantity for my budget. After searching for months and months, I decided that I would just do it myself. I had never even sewn a button on before, so being the one to physically make the swimwear probably wasn't the best option— but I did have a friend, Bec, who liked to make her own dresses. I messaged Bec to see if she was interested, and she said, "Sure, let's do it."

I remember thinking, *Swimwear can't be too hard to make*— oh, how I was wrong. Lycra is a lot trickier to work with than dress fabrics and you need a different machine to make it happen. These machines are expensive, as is labor in Australia. We learned all of this over the next year.

I spent about $5000 setting up a manufacturing studio for Bec and we just began with trial and error. It took a while, but we finally got the first collection finished on the day of our launch party. It was the first time I saw the whole collection and held it in my hands. To see it on the models that night was another one of those moments that gives me a wave of pride.

I was very proud of the brand that Mae by Tyler had evolved into. We were extremely ethical and sustainable, and completely Australian-made. The brand had successfully expanded into swimwear, and we were starting to get some traction. In 2019, I applied for a spot at Mercedes-Benz Fashion Week. I honestly didn't think I would get it; we were a small brand, and Fashion Week is huge. I was so used to rejection by that point—as a lot of small business owners, models, and entrepreneurs are—that I was genuinely shocked when I got the call to say they were offering me a stall. The stall cost me $2000—not including flights to Sydney and accommodation—but it was open to the public so I could make sales over the two days. At the time, $2000 was a lot for my little brand, but I knew I would regret not going, so I signed the contract.

Even though I had broken my leg five weeks beforehand in a surfing accident and was on crutches, which made everything that little bit harder, Fashion Week was amazing. I took my younger cousin Tatum with me to help, and it was four of the best days I've had in business. It opened a whole new world up to me. I'd come so far in three years from my humble beginnings selling handmade rings out of a shoebox at College Lawn.

I felt another one of those waves of pride when I came back to Perth afterward. It was the same feeling I'd had sitting in that boardroom, designing my website. Those moments in life and business are so important. They're like my little gold nuggets that make the effort worth the self-doubt, anxieties, and feelings of failure on the way.

I rarely felt truly accomplished—or I rarely *let* myself feel accomplished. Even though I was doing all these cool things, I still felt like I was failing. When I told strangers what I did, they would say things like "Wow! That's amazing!" and in my head I would just think, *Not that amazing, because it's not working.*

I didn't feel proud of my work for a long time because one major indicator of success was missing: money. I was still working for someone else at the bar, I didn't make enough money with Mae by Tyler to pay myself a decent wage, and my savings account was far from huge. So despite all the cool things I was doing, I felt like a failure.

I had tied success and money so closely together in my mind that no matter what I achieved, it wasn't enough. Kylie Jenner could have worn my jewelry, but if I had still been working at that bar, it would not have counted as a win. It took me years to rewire my brain to redefine success, but I'm glad I did. I think having that mindset risks you missing some of your greatest achievements.

Around this time, I also launched my vegan catering business, The Platter Club. One day, I saw someone had posted to a Perth Facebook group wanting a vegan grazing table for their wedding. It was quite clear to me that there was no caterer in Perth that was solely vegan and nailing it; I saw the post and thought, *I could do that*. So I took that day off my bar job and started the business. I'd heard that for a business to succeed, it had to be the first, something different or the best. I knew I was the first, so I was sure I was on to my next million-dollar business idea. I loved Mae by Tyler, but at the end of the day I wanted to be an entrepreneur and The Platter Club gave me that opportunity. My plan was to get it off the ground and make my income from that and Mae by Tyler, so I could quit the bar job.

Working in hospitality for so long gave me a lot of insight into food handling and the legalities involved, as well as food photography. Mae by Tyler had given me knowledge of marketing and business legalities, so I had a head start there too.

I spent that day off work driving around to the food stores in Perth that stocked the best vegan meats and cheeses. I didn't want the grazing tables and other products to have just fruit and vegetables; I really wanted them to be full of delicious food that nonvegans would eat and be impressed by. Max and I were still very tight on cash at this point, so I did my best to also use food from the fridge and save where I could.

Once I had grabbed the food samples, I went around to op shops and chose table decor. I also went to the industrial area, found a cardboard box supplier to make mini grazing boxes, and bought fifty of them. The next steps were to create the business name, register it, and make its social media accounts. I smashed all that out by lunchtime, so I then spent a couple of hours creating different grazing boxes to photograph for Instagram.

I was set to open for business, and I had it all done by teatime for only $150.

Over the next couple of weeks, I would keep making grazing boxes and smashing out content for The Platter Club's Instagram and Facebook pages. I had "vegan cheese connoisseur" in our Instagram bio, and made a big effort to promote the fact we offered amazing vegan cheese and meats. The no-rabbit-food approach helped a lot, because vegan alternatives were gaining traction at the time. I was very good at marketing the business and we got very busy; I was posting in all of the vegan Facebook pages and made sure the brand was right on trend. Within the first month, we had 800 Instagram followers and two weddings booked. I went out for lunch with the first bride and brought her a selection of vegan meats and cheeses to try, because I knew wedding cake businesses gave out samples. The bride was very impressed.

I completely winged that meeting and just said yes with a big smile on my face to everything she wanted. I wasn't concerned about making a profit from the first wedding. I just wanted my costs covered. More importantly at that point: the job would give me experience, credibility, and content for the socials.

Although I had worked as a function manager, I had never catered a wedding—so I knew I needed to nail the amount of food I provided to build my brand's reputation. I rang five grazing-table businesses around Australia pretending to be a bride, and asked them everything I needed to know. How much per head? How many loaves of bread? How much food does each guest get to eat? How long does it take you to set up? How long can the food sit there for? What was popular with other brides? It was a bit cheeky, but it meant I was going in prepared.

I did a trial run mini-grazer with my friends before the first wedding and felt confident. On the day-of, I "hired" my best friend to come and help me (she wouldn't let me pay her—my friends and family are honestly the backbone of any business venture I have had) and we smashed out the grazer with time to spare.

It was a hit. The only feedback I got was that we needed more carbs, but other than that, it went really well. I definitely didn't make any money that day, but the content I got from that job helped me book multiple weddings in the months to follow.

Unsurprisingly, I was extremely busy between juggling work full-time at the bar, Mae by Tyler, and The Platter Club. As The Platter Club started to grow, so did my legal obligations. I had to jump through multiple hoops to get the required certifications. Business can be very intense and now when I feel overwhelmed by obstacles, I write a list and take it one step at a time, doing everything in my power to cross off each step.

My end goal was to run this catering business, and one of the obstacles along the way was getting health and safety approval for my at-home kitchen. I fought for months and months, but in the end I realized that a better option was to go around that hurdle and register my business in a commercial kitchen down the road. Yes, it would have been cheaper and more convenient to use my own kitchen, but at the end of the day my goal was to keep that business running, and that meant picking my battles. It's a very good skill to have: knowing when to fight and chase for something, and when to let it go.

Another time, I decided to create ready-to-eat portable grazing boxes to feed twenty to thirty people. These boxes could be made at my kitchen and then dropped off at events, so I didn't have to prep at the event. I had my heart set on buying some wooden boxes from a business in the eastern states. The boxes were handmade and so beautiful; they were perfect.

After weeks of trying to find a courier to transport them to Western Australia for a reasonable price, I had to give up on those exact wooden boxes to stay within my budget. I knew that I really wanted to offer that service, though, so instead of jumping over the transport hurdle I went around it, and made the boxes myself. Well, my family did—again, they have always been my biggest supporters.

The Platter Club was going so well that I was doing weddings and engagement parties. The prep was enormous but I loved it. I found an amazing business partner, Llyrus, who had a vegan dessert catering company, and we just clicked. Together, we started our events company Forward Management, which was so exciting. I had always worked in events, but they were finally going to be mine. Our first event was called The Vegan Girls' Night Out. It was booked in for the week after I took Mae by Tyler to Fashion Week, and I was still working as a bar manager with full-time hours.

Planning that with Llyrus was some of the best fun I have had. I oversaw finding sponsors, so I put together a sponsorship package and pulled in some big names. My background in events helped me write up these packages because I knew what they needed to look like, and I knew how to use free graphic design tools like Canva. I then cold-called big businesses and asked them what they wanted from a small business when they considered sponsorship. I wrote a lot of notes and made sure the sponsors were getting something in return; it definitely helped that both Llyrus and I had grown a loyal Instagram following, which we used as leverage.

We posted our sponsors all over our socials, mentioned them at the event, put flyers in the gift bags, and gave them free tickets to future Forward Management events for them to give away on their own socials. It was a very different audience from my *Aussie Gold Hunters* demographic, so although I had a small social following on my personal Instagram, it was the follows on my business page that the sponsors were interested in.

We ended up getting around $6000 worth of sponsorships from names like Bio Cheese, Beyond Meat, Brookie's Byron Dry Gin, and Funk Cider. We marketed the hell out of it. Tickets to The Vegan Girls' Night Out were $70 a pop and it was a sell-out event. We catered it ourselves, had stalls, guest speakers, and live music. The guest speakers were all local women who owned vegan businesses, and it was a great opportunity for them to tell their stories and get exposure for their brands.

I hosted the guest speakers with zero experience—another time that having abundant self-confidence came in handy. I was nervous to host, but every time a negative thought came into my brain, I reminded myself that I could do it. It seems clichéd, but positive self-talk always helps.

It was such a fun night but such a huge effort; we stayed until 2 a.m. on clean-up. My family and friends were the people who made that event happen. The support from Mum, Aunty Sha, and everyone else carried the event. Llyrus and I came up with the ideas, but without my friends and family working ten-hour shifts with no pay, the event would have failed. I am so privileged to have family that has my back at every turn.

Aussie Gold Hunters was also giving me a fair bit of social media exposure, which meant I was getting an influx of people contacting me on Facebook and Instagram wanting to learn how to find gold. I saw the opportunity and took it. I love all my businesses, but I would say I am an opportunistic entrepreneur—I see a way to make money and I make it happen.

You see, you can't go to school to become a gold prospector: it's all knowledge and experience, something my family had accrued plenty of over the generations. The thought of losing all that priceless information scared me. I wanted to share our secrets with as many people as possible to ensure the art of true gold prospecting never died.

I was on my lunch break at the bar, sitting in the car park eating a bowl of chips and thinking about this when it hit me. I was going to start a club with paid memberships so I could teach people how to become gold prospectors. I rang Mum and Dad. They loved this idea too, and were as supportive as ever; they also wanted to generously preserve their knowledge for others to enjoy. Within two weeks I launched The Prospectors Club (yes, a similar name to The Platter

Club).

I wasn't getting into credit card debt again, though—I designed the logo, website, and membership platform all by myself. If I didn't know how to do something, I googled it. I was still broke, so I only hired help if I still couldn't work out how to do it after hopping on Google, and if I could truly afford it and knew it would save time. Now I can afford to outsource a lot more, and that's a luxury I didn't have at the start.

The Club took off and I had twenty paying members in a week. Another wave of pride coursed through me, and this time I really felt it because financially we were in the green hard and fast. I was living away from the Goldfields still, so, often at night, I would drive my little Mazda 3 the whole fourteen-hour trip home—200 kilometers of which was a gravel road with zero reception. I was determined to get content for the Club and go prospecting, and I couldn't do either if I was in Perth.

It goes without saying Mum and Dad were the knowledge. Everything I teach is from them; The Prospectors Club *is* them. I am just the one who knows how to share it on MailChimp and Facebook. They were working up in the Murchison, so sometimes I would do twenty-hour round trips on my days off. I am proud of twenty-three-year-old Tyler for that; she would eventually reap the reward for her effort.

My tone of voice for The Prospectors Club was very different from that of my other businesses. It was much more me, much more laidback; I spoke to my members as friends and family, because that's how I saw them. I realized quickly that not only did a business tone *not* strengthen those relationships, but the personal relationship was what made the Club great. Members signed up for the content but stayed for the community. Again, I realized that being myself paid off.

By that point it was mid-2019. I was *still* running Mae by Tyler, the catering and events business, and The Prospectors Club, as well as working at the bar. It was not sustainable, but I just wasn't earning enough from the three businesses to leave the bar. I had cut back my hours a lot, but I couldn't pull the pin completely, which really impacted my mental health and self-worth. I felt like a failure in business every time I turned up to my shift at that bar. Why was I still not good enough to work for myself? I was only twenty-three, but I felt like a horrible entrepreneur.

A couple of months later, after a year of being in the swimwear business with Bec, she decided to move on from my label and branch out into her own thing. While I was so excited for her, it did mean I had to find another manufacturer, which proved too big a challenge. I closed Mae by Tyler, my firstborn business. It was one of the hardest decisions I have ever made.

Then, when we were about to start filming *Aussie Gold Hunters* for my third season, Mum and Dad called me to say they wanted to pull the pin on it. I tried to convince Mum and Dad to sign the contract with me, but I could tell they were done. Financially, that hurt. The show was the one thing each year that allowed me to get in front and put a good chunk of cash in my savings. I was also starting to appreciate what *Aussie Gold Hunters* was doing for my social media presence, which I really wanted to grow. Meanwhile, Llyrus, my business partner for Forward Management, was also going through some hard times—so we had put a hold on that too. It seemed like everything I had been working toward in my career was ending.

That familiar darkness started to descend on me—that feeling of helplessness so intense that I couldn't imagine ever feeling normal again. My depression had stormed back in. I don't think it was necessarily triggered by what was going on in my life; it had been sitting there staring at me, unacknowledged, for the past six months. Therapy and medication helped, but I'd abandoned those; having so much on had meant I was able to keep my mental health issues at bay. It's like I had been treading water and it was just there, tugging me down slowly as I focused on just keeping my head above the surface. Once I felt like all my hard work on my career was slipping away, the depression grabbed me by the ankles and pulled me under. No matter what I did each day, I could not keep my head above water anymore.

On a logical level, I actually felt quite positive about my career. I knew it would be okay—I would work it out and the universe would have my back, like it always does—but I just couldn't seem to tell my brain that. It's bizarre to know you are fine, but not feel it at all.

Around this time, I was very drunk at a music festival when my best friend and I got into a slight argument over nothing—but that was enough to set me off. I ran out of the festival without telling anyone and straight into the surrounding bushland. I had a million thoughts rushing through my mind, but the loudest was the one wanting everything to stop.

I went into that bushland, drunk, by myself, and looking for trouble that night. I wanted to find someone who would end it all for me because I was too cowardly to do it myself. I was begging the universe to let me walk into danger. I kept walking into the bush, deeper and deeper, trying to find someone who would hurt me. I wanted to hurt myself. I just kept crying and walking around, searching for the bad guy parents warn their children about. He wasn't there; instead, I sat in the middle of the bush by myself, crying. There was no sense of tomorrow, no ability to see beyond those feelings, and no real appreciation of the severity of death, but I truly believed it was the only way out. Anything was better than staying with my thoughts.

Eventually, I got a taxi home, grabbed a coat, and started walking the streets of my neighborhood, still crying, again trying to find someone who would make my pain physical. If the pain was tangible, it would make sense in my mind and I could allow myself to be upset. Either that, or someone would just end it all for me. Once again, though, he wasn't there.

I have walked the streets at night a few times since, in a better frame of mind and doing everything I possibly can to avoid trouble, and still I always run into creepy men lurking about. That night I was actively searching for danger, and the universe would not give it to me. I am thankful now it kept the streets safe for me.

After walking around for a while, I took myself home. I was beyond sad—it was a feeling of complete misery, despair, hopelessness, recklessness, impulsiveness, and carelessness. It was a recipe for disaster. I grabbed the sharpest knife I could find and, for the first time ever, started cutting my legs.

It was instant relief, and for the first time all the voices started to calm and quiet down. That was the start of my self-harm craving. Self-harming for me became like taking a Panadol for a headache or a QuickEze for indigestion; it was the one thing that could shut up the intrusive thoughts. It was a mixture of self-destruction and validation. I spent so many years in denial about my mental pain that as soon as I made it physical, it was validated. It was like I finally had cold hard evidence that there was something wrong: *Look, I have scars. That proves I am fucked in the head.*

Max came home that night to a scene I imagine would have been hard to process: blood was everywhere and I had stabbed the knife into our couch. He was a mixture of shocked, mad, and overwhelmed. Like most people in such a situation, he didn't know what to do.

I should have been admitted to a psychology ward at this point. That episode was very out of character. The cuts were almost my attempt at begging for someone to realize I needed serious help. I don't blame anyone for this except myself; it wasn't the people around me who needed to force me into a psych ward. I needed to do that myself, but I just didn't know how. Maybe if Max had been better educated about mental health, he would have seen the warning signs—but at the end of the day I am responsible for my mental health and I should have got help sooner.

The actual cuts were not deep. They would eventually heal and be gone from my skin forever, but my psychological state was not something that would heal naturally with time. Max put me in bed and said to me, "I can't do this anymore; you need to go home to your parents so they can help you."

It was a stab in the guts. I don't blame him, though; he had been thrown in the deep end. For some reason, I thought that because I had stood by him, with his mental illness, for so long, he would know how to do the same for me—but he didn't. I had never felt so alone, and his words marked the beginning of our relationship breakdown.

The trouble with me going home and telling my parents, or anyone in my life, was that I had completely sheltered them from what was happening with my mental health. I had not told a single soul besides Max about my diagnosis; I was so embarrassed that I couldn't say it out loud. It was so much easier to keep my mouth shut than to try to explain what was happening. I just couldn't be bothered, and it was easier to act okay than to deal with it.

Of course, it did get to the point where I needed to tell the people around me. Fortunately for me, my best friend Sarah had a lot of experience with mental health issues and was the person who helped the most. She saw the self-harm as a cry for help and became the person I went to for support. She never judged me, thought I was a burden or saw me as unstable. Having someone who unconditionally had my back like that was the light shining in the dark. I also had my two other best friends, Sophie and Kyah, who made me feel loved when I didn't love myself. Cherishing those three friendships will always be my top priority because they were, and are, my safety net.

I don't know why I was so petrified to tell my parents—they are extremely supportive. I think it was partly because I was still finding it very hard to show pain and vulnerability to my family, and partly because if I told the people closest to me it would make it real. Plus,

I knew they would ask me all about it, which was a conversation I didn't want to have. Again, it was so much easier to try to pretend like it didn't exist. Eventually, though, the truth will out.

It happened one day when my Dad and I got into a huge fight. I'm a copy-paste of Dad when it comes to stubbornness and slight anger issues, so when we fight, we really fight. It always makes me laugh; he really has raised a little version of himself. He always taught me to not take shit, to stand up for myself, and not back down; now he has to deal with the person he created.

When the fight heated up, I cracked. I just blurted out, "I have bipolar!" in a river of tears. It was my way of saying "Please, give me a break. I need help." From that moment on, my parents have been nothing but supportive, patient, understanding, and gentle. It has taken some learning, but I know for a fact that if it wasn't for the support network around me, I would not be here today.

My heart sinks when I see people take their own lives or turn to addiction because of mental illness. I know that would absolutely have been me if it wasn't for the people around me. I am not any braver, stronger, or more resilient than those people who lost their battles; I am just blessed to have had enough people to catch me when I was trying to jump. Others are not that lucky.

Over the next year or so, things would get progressively worse before they got better. Although some amazing opportunities came my way, I also went through massive changes and real lows. I landed my dream job on another TV show two weeks after I self-harmed for the first time. I was working at the bar—having gone back to hospitality to supplement my income from The Prospectors Club—when I missed a call from our family friend, who had been a director on *Aussie Gold Hunters*. He had rung to gauge my interest in appearing on a show following an American named Parker Schnabel and his quest to trace gold rush routes across the globe, uncovering treasure on the way.

I was keen for anything. I am so lucky that this friend had my back and pushed to have me on the show. If it wasn't for him, I would never have had the opportunity. I still had to go through an audition process, just so the high ups could make sure I wasn't a dud, but within two weeks of that phone call, I was on a plane to Canada to meet Parker. Not even a month later, we were on the road filming *Gold Rush: Parker's Trail*—a pretty big TV show.

I decided to completely bury that I had self-harmed, and got on with my new job. So much of my self-worth was tied to my work and, in the name of succeeding at it, I have an innate ability to act completely sane through some of my most unstable times. Having so much of my self-worth tied to my career is not necessarily a good thing—it's in fact something I'm trying to unlearn. One perk of this ability to mask my symptoms, however, is that my mental illness has impacted my career so minimally that colleagues would have had zero idea about the horrific depressive episode I was coming out of. That wasn't because we weren't close, or because they didn't care, but because I was so good at saving face. I was afraid my mental illness would ruin the thing I cared for the most. It was almost like living a double life. I'd always get told, "Oh, wow. I would have no idea you were going through that," and that was because I did everything in my power to make sure they didn't.

The following months were a complete blur. Once I left Perth to film the TV show, Max and I broke up. I spent what felt like a whole lifetime with a person who became a stranger overnight. We had grown up together, moved in together at seventeen, and gone through life lessons and turmoils together that many couples don't experience in a lifetime.

The person who was once half of my personality was gone, and I was left wondering how I could possibly feel emotions without someone else dictating them. Max and I had been through so much that I tied my happiness to his. After seeing him so low for so long, his happiness had become mine, and his sadness had become my anxiety. If he was okay, I was okay, and if he wasn't it was my job to fix it. The moment I noticed a slight change in his energy my anxiety would spike. *What have I done? What do I do to fix it? Why will he not talk?* I'd obsess, and in would come the clinginess and worry until his energy returned to normal. Two years later, I'm still trying to unlearn that codependency.

As hard as a breakup is, and as much as I do cherish that relationship, ending it was the best thing to ever happen to me. I had to learn to be alone, I had to learn to nurture my sense of self, I had to learn true self-love, and I had to learn to insist on a better partner for myself.

All these feelings were put on hold, though, because I set off to travel Australia filming an international TV show. My mind put the breakup on pause. It wasn't a conscious decision, but my brain would not allow me to process the breakup or feel any emotions from it just yet. It was the end of a seven-year relationship, and the only time I cried was out of guilt when my ex called in tears.

I left him during an emotional storm to travel the country and I will always carry some guilt for that. I would try my hardest at night to sit down and process what was happening, but my brain would not let me. I would do my best to grasp my emotions about the situation, but just sit there, blank. My brain was dissociating as a coping mechanism and there was nothing I could do about it.

It did work, though: I got through the trip with no major breakdowns. It was seamless, and I had the time of my life—but a lot would change when I got back to reality and had my old life to deal with.

I started seeing someone new straight after the breakup because I had a hole I needed to fill. I preferred to be with someone who did not fill my emotional needs, who did not treat me well, over having to be alone with myself.

I wish I could go back and tell myself to lean into solitude—and even learn to love it—because until I did, I would have settled for anyone who could help me escape it. I wish I had learned self-love, so I didn't go searching high and low for someone else to fill that void. I had to learn these lessons the hard way, and created a mess because of it.

With the benefit of hindsight, I can see that something pretty spectacular emerged from the rubble of that period in my life. It was another butterfly effect in action, and this chain reaction affirmed my belief that things exit my life to create space for what's truly meant for me. Suddenly everything made sense: the businesses not moving forward, Max and I separating, losing my spot with *Aussie Gold Hunters*.

Parker's Trail came at the perfect time and, in a way, it saved me.

12

MY GOLD RUSH

I have met many interesting characters on my life's travels, and I met some of my very favorites on my three-month road trip around Australia filming *Gold Rush: Parker's Trail.*

Those were some of the best times I have had in my short twenty-seven years. Like everything I have done in my life, my highlights were the people I met and the places I went. I get weirdly attached to both. I don't know if it's them or the emotions they bring up. When I have really struggled with my mental illness, truly feeling emotions has been a struggle; the sentimental attachments I form are all the more precious to me because of that.

Australia is an amazing country, and I got to visit places full of heart and character that aren't normally on the tourism ads—when you're hunting for gold, you must go off the beaten track. After all, as Dad always says: if finding gold was easy, everyone would be doing it.

Parker's Trail was a spin-off of the original American show *Gold Rush*, where Parker made his name. On our show, I was going to be Parker's prospecting guide Down Under. We would be joined by Fred, a veteran turned gold miner and one of Parker's best friends, and Danny, the amazing cameraman who would join us on adventures to support and film us.

Followed by a huge crew, we would be on the hunt for gold and potential leases for Parker to buy in Australia. As the resident Aussie, I would have to use my local knowledge and contacts to find Parker ground that would make money.

To be honest, I was extremely nervous. I had been thrown into a job with a huge amount of responsibility and my performance would be aired to hundreds of thousands of people around the world. I wanted to impress Parker and make sure I did the job I was hired to do.

I didn't have much time to really think about what I was getting into, so I fell back on one of my favorite mottos: I walked through the door that had opened for me, and decided to figure out the rest later. If I had really known the intense expectations of the job before I left, I might have second-guessed my abilities to do it. In a way I'm glad I went in a little naive.

The job itself wasn't the only thing I rushed into headlong. When Parker landed in Melbourne, we hit it off instantly. We had such similar interests and humor; conversation and being around each other felt very natural. I felt like I had known him for much longer than I actually had, so things naturally progressed—what started off as a friendship quickly grew into an intimate relationship, expedited by the fact that we were living and working on a TV show together.

The sneaking began the moment we started filming in Melbourne. To make sure no one knew what was happening between us, sneaking into each other's rooms or swags at night and sneaking back before the crack of dawn was our new norm. We hid the relationship so well because we wanted to avoid intertwining our professional and personal lives. This is a very difficult skill to master in a normal working environment, let alone when you are both barely in your mid-twenties and spending 24/7 with each other!

As you can imagine, taking things slow wasn't an option. Not that this bothered me—the fun of a new relationship, especially one that came with extra "excitement," was a welcome distraction from my below-average mental health. It gave new life to my happy hormone receptors, something that I hadn't been able to do by myself for a long time. Of course, I don't think romance should ever be a bandaid for mental health woes—but having some light come into your life at dark times can make it easier for you to find the bandaids yourself.

Parker's Trail was a wild experience for a twenty-three-year-old from the bush. I had done TV work before with *Aussie Gold Hunters*, but this was like that on steroids. The film crew had twenty people instead of just three, the budget was much bigger, and the places we visited were much more extreme.

Adding to that was our tight schedule. Australia is massive, and we had three months to travel the whole country in a Toyota HiLux. It was the middle of the Australian summer, so we didn't see the temperature drop below 95 degrees Fahrenheit. It was normal to spend weeks at 100 degrees Fahrenheit and above; we even had days when it would hit 120 degrees in the sun. Plus, the four of us were living and working together in extreme conditions and locations, always being filmed and wearing a mic around our necks. It was rough, but all of that I could handle. The most horrific part was actually the flies.

I am a girl from the bush—I can do flies—but this was next level. Millions of flies constantly all over your face, buzzing in your ears, poking your eyes—it was horrible. Then there was the persistent threat of the harsh sun, deadly snakes, spiders, crocodiles, and other typically terrifying Aussie fauna. It was a lot. I tried to warn the team about the heat and flies before they got here, but I don't think any warning can really prepare you for the outback in summer.

Our first stop eased the boys into a typical Australian summer. We kicked things off in Victoria, which was the least extreme place we visited. The Golden Triangle—the region stretching between Ballarat, Wedderburn, and Bendigo—was one of our first stops on our prospecting journey around Australia, and it was a great way to introduce the team to the Australian gold scene and what it's known best for: big gold nuggets.

Once we hit the Golden Triangle, I took the boys to where the Welcome Stranger was found. The Welcome Stranger is the biggest gold nugget to have ever been found in the world and has a current gold weight value of $5.9 million. These days, a nugget that size would fetch a much higher premium than just the weight value, which is only based off what the current price is per ounce. A nugget like this would be worth much more due to its rarity.

I showed them a replica of the Welcome Stranger for some inspiration; I wanted the boys to see what we Aussies do best. In the Yukon, Canada, where Parker and Fred mined, they'd find placer gold (small particles) in the form of fines. Gold nuggets over 10 grams would have been on the rarer side, let alone gold nuggets over an ounce, which the Golden Triangle is known for. The replica was huge and barely liftable, even though it was only a fraction of the real 72-kilogram mammoth.

Once I had shown the boys Victoria's potential—very optimistic to hope to ever match the Welcome Stranger but, hey, it got them excited—I wanted to prove to them that prospectors were still killing it out there, so I introduced them to Ian Holland. Ian mines shallow leads in Victoria—alluvial washes following old rivers, something the region is known for.

I felt the need to show Parker that mining in Australia was sustainable, and Ian was the perfect guy. Ian began prospecting as a young boy and loved it, making good money by the time he was a young man. He said he'd always planned to leave prospecting and get a "real job" the day he made less money prospecting than he would on a salary. Fifty years later that day has never come, and he is still doing what he knows best. I take my hat off to any full-time prospector who can make a living and support a family; it's not an easy feat.

Ian is a rare breed in the gold world: honest and willing to share his knowledge. He welcomed us straight away, and we camped in a green field next to a full river under the stars. With a fire crackling and some of Ian's home-brewed beer sitting in our bellies, it was perfect.

We sat around the fire that night teaching the Poms and the Yanks about Aussie rhyming slang, like what "dead horse on your snag" means, and Ian showed us some of his gold. Very fortunately for me, Ian made me look good and whipped out two huge nuggets—one was 70 ounces, and the other was 30 ounces. Life-changing pieces for any prospector. He was my contact, and he was the real deal.

These were some of the biggest gold nuggets the boys had seen, and much bigger than my biggest nugget. I remember the boys saying that night, "Well, at least we are in the right spot," and I went to bed knowing I had done my job properly—for the time being, at least.

The next day we got up to see what Ian's site had to offer, and had a couple of hiccups. We needed to test the ground to see if it was viable to buy for Parker. It was all well and good holding a couple of big nuggets, but the ground needed to be producing good gold in front of their eyes to really impress.

Of course, the loader and excavator broke down. Typical. Any gold prospector will tell you that if something can go wrong out bush, it will. Parker helped with the repairs and we ended up getting to sample a fair amount of dirt. We then processed the dirt through a little wet plant that Fred and I had purchased, which was a stressful moment.

Parker had given me a budget to buy a portable wet plant for us to take around Australia to test the ground. I had to choose between an older, cheaper machine and a newer one that was way over budget. I went with the older one, and in hindsight wish I could tell past Tyler to not be a fucking stinge considering what would end up happening to it.

Parker then panned off the ground we'd processed. It was his first time using the wet plant and his first time testing ground in Australia for alluvial finds. If the pan was empty, I would look like an idiot—or at least a shitty prospector—on international television.

Parker panned off the dirt and looked up.

Parker is the king of poker faces, and I could never tell if he was ecstatic or if I was about to be fired. He looked at Danny and said, "Are you filming? You're going to want to get this." Ian was standing there too, also nervous and feeling the pressure. He'd said his ground was good, and it wouldn't be the best look if the pan was empty.

I remember thinking, *Okay, Tyler, if the pan is empty, it's going to be okay. There are other options. It's just one pan. We can test other areas. We still have more time to test here. It's shit, but that's how prospecting is.*

Parker flipped the pan for me to see, and there it was: gold. We all looked at each other and went, "No fucking way." It was one of the best samples Parker had ever seen, and double the size of samples he would get in the Yukon. There was a gram in the pan—an amazing result—and in the blink of the eye I had both proven the legitimacy of my contacts and that Ian had buyable, sustainable ground.

Parker and the boys were impressed. The lease was for sale, it had gold and was ready to go. The area was very small compared to what Parker was used to, but it was a very good start. Parker was extremely interested in doing more testing on the area, but the issue was time. I had set up contacts all around Australia to meet us on certain days and Victoria was only our first stop.

I could have risked fucking up our schedule from the start and missing out on seeing the other potentially incredible spots, but it wouldn't have been right by my contacts. The prospectors we were going to see didn't care that we were filming a TV show, but I'd said I would get there and I wanted to keep my word. Plus, I truly believed we could do better. That ground was great, but it wasn't worth derailing the trip to stay and test more on the first place we saw.

Then, doubt started to creep in. *Why don't we just stay in Victoria, test more ground, continue to pursue that area and run with it?* It would have saved money and time, and I would have delivered a guaranteed good result for Parker. Why bother taking him there if we were going to just leave after getting a good test? I didn't want to be the one making the call, but I was the one who had planned out the rest of our trip. If I believed in those next places, I needed to back myself, as I could practically hear my dad saying.

We also had producers advising us that we had a show to make and needed to keep going. So I trusted my abilities and said, "Let's keep moving. I know it's great, but I promise you, we will find better."

So now I had just made a promise on international TV that we would find better ground than that—how clever! It's a fine line between arrogance and backing yourself sometimes. Nevertheless, the boys agreed and we said goodbye to the green fields and golden pans of Victoria to head toward the better things I'd so boldly promised.

We set off 3000 kilometers north to the Palmer River, an extremely remote location in Far North Queensland (FNQ). The Palmer is the wild west of the north. It's very rich, harsh terrain, and for every ounce of gold in the hills, there are a hundred secrets to uncover too.

I'm from the outback, and I can confidently say people living in FNQ are a different breed in the best way possible. I fell in love with the history, the people, the gold, and the stories. When you tell outsiders you are going there, they say, "Be careful and be prepared. That's a wild place."

The longer I stayed there, the more I realized just how wild it was. It's the kind of place where you'll be shot if you end up in the wrong area. Out there, your only chance of surviving a snake bite is a mercy flight with the Royal Flying Doctors, and the only way in or out in peak wet season is by chopper. You must truly love isolation to live there.

I met some absolute characters in FNQ and created some truly great memories, but the gold was what made FNQ the best stop on the trip for the boys and me. I was gobsmacked by the amount coming out at the next lease we saw; it was better than I had expected. I knew that if we could get the owners to consider selling, I had a shot at making good on the promise I'd made in Victoria.

We pulled up at the Fitzgeralds' lease after a much longer-than-needed drive. I had got everybody a little lost because the boys made me navigate our way through ridges, hills, and gullies on tiny off-road tracks, even though I'd said from the start that I suck with directions.

Anyway, we got there in the end, and we met the Fitzgeralds at one of their sites. They are a huge mining family in the Palmer River with a monopoly on the local goldfields. If you want to get into mining in the Palmer, you need to get in with the Fitzgeralds. There are five generations of them mining in the area—and they are an extremely tight-knit family who stay close to one another and rarely let outsiders in.

I knew it was going to be an extremely hard job to earn their trust, and it certainly didn't help that we were rocking up with a twenty-person film crew. Gaining their confidence was paramount if we wanted any chance of getting access to the extremely rich riverbeds of the Palmer.

The introductions went well; they let us watch a clean-up of one of their wet plants pretty much off the bat. I was impressed that they let us do that, especially with a film crew around. It's an intrusive part of the process to see, but I think we all clicked quickly, and Parker made them feel comfortable.

The good thing about FNQ was that, of all of Australia, the gold there was the most like the Yukon, where Parker mined. It's the only place in the country where the gold acted like his, and so the mining techniques were the same. I think it made him feel comfortable; he spoke the language, and could draw easy comparisons to his ground. It wasn't too far beyond his comfort zone.

Leading the Fitzgerald family were Cheryl and Jack, both in their seventies. Armed with wisdom, experience and knowledge, they had created a spectacular life in the Palmer. They headed the clan, and were surrounded by their kids and grandkids, with a lot of them following the mining tradition and working their own claims and mine sites close by.

Cheryl, the matriarch of the family, is a tough, incredible woman who can boast a well-lived life and a deep understanding of the gold world. She's someone I instantly admired. I felt an immediate desire to please her and gain her acceptance. She and Jack, along with other members of the family, were there for the clean-up.

We went over the wet plant and just from the sluice alone, which doesn't include any of the larger detectable nuggets going out the oversized, we got a glimpse at just how rich those riverbeds were.

At the top of the sluice, a trough through which water and paydirt are poured, there is a mechanism that sorts the gold into size: fines, smaller rocks and gold go into the sluice, where the heavier gold sinks to the bottom while the dirt is washed away, and larger pieces fall into the oversized. The sluice was filled with the shiny stuff and I was so relieved to see it. Once again, it was a weight off my shoulders seeing good gold straight off the bat.

We still had to weigh the nuggets that came out of the oversize, pan off the sluice fines, do a total weigh up, and compare it to how much ground was mined that day to get an accurate test result for Parker. That way, he could assess it in line with his budget and see much the ground was worth per tonne (the Aussie way) and per foot (the American/Canadian way).

After a day of testing, we finally got back to Cheryl and Jack's beautiful property to do the weigh up. I was a little anxious to see Parker's reaction. I was hoping the Palmer would make all the risks worth it and that there would be enough gold there to get everyone excited about Australia again. Thankfully, when the gold was plopped onto the scales, a smile lit up every face.

The weigh up was a success. From memory, they got 7 ounces— and the wet plant hadn't even run all day. It was a lot more gold per square foot than Parker had ever seen in the Yukon. Sure, there wasn't as much ground, and it was a little more sporadic, but it was a very good result. We still had a lot of testing to do, and we still had to figure out if the Fitzgeralds even wanted to sell the good ground— but the Palmer was officially off to a flying start.

The rest of the night was so beautiful. The Fitzgeralds had built a little oasis in the middle of the outback: a beautiful open-walled house, equipped with an outdoor shower and a freshwater dam for swimming, surrounded by fruit trees and green grass with the hospitality to match.

We swam in the dam and showered outside, and the Fitzgeralds served us all a beautiful homecooked meal. It was bliss. That night we camped under the stars in a swag, and I wrote in my notebook that I felt very content.

We spent about five days with the Fitzgeralds testing, mining, and getting our hands dirty with various family members. On one of the days, I was assigned loader driver at one of the sites. I had been driving a loader for a while by that point, but solely for scrape and detect, the type of mining we do in Western Australia. I hadn't done much actual loading with one.

My job was to pick up the oversized piles from the wet plant, carry them to an open pad, and lay down the rocks evenly in a long strip. It sounds easy enough, but it required a fair amount of skill— plus I had to maneuver the loader through a thin passageway. On one side was a big drop off into a dam and on the other was the pipe feeding the wet plant. If I fucked up and went right, I would have cut off water supply to their operation, costing them a lot of money. If I went left, well, I would probably die and completely write off their very pricey loader—so, no pressure. I also had Cheryl, Jack, and Parker watching to make sure I didn't fuck it up, and, of course, a whole film crew filming it for international television. A walk in the park really!

I got the job done and I learned a lot about operating that day. Cheryl came up to me afterward and said, "I trust any chick that can drive a loader." I felt like I'd really nailed what I'd come to do.

We spent some more time with the Fitzgeralds, and I loved every moment of it. Parker was happy with the contacts and the ground, convinced that the Palmer had sufficient mining potential.

I was happy to move on from the Palmer knowing that if we didn't come across anything better, at least we had this option. The way the Fitzgeralds talked about the ground and the gold really resonated with me. Cheryl and Jack never overmined the area and they only took what they needed. They called the riverbank their "bank"; when they needed some cash, they would do some mining and once they had enough gold out to get by, they would stop. They didn't rape and pillage the ground, and they were adamant about leaving enough gold in the ground for future generations.

To them, gold mining wasn't about becoming a millionaire—it was a way of life that they loved. If the sun was shining, they would knock off work at ten and go barra fishing. If they wanted a week off and the bills were paid, they would take a week off. They reminded me a lot of my parents, who also prospect for the lifestyle and not the money.

As we packed up our swags, I felt like I had made a new family, created lasting relationships, learned a lot about gold mining, and done a good job. I left the Palmer feeling very content, blissfully unaware that our next stop, Halls Creek, would be an absolute shitshow.

One of the most memorable characters from my time in FNQ was Magoo, the barefoot pilot. I met him while staying with the

Fitzgeralds. I have met some quirky bushmen, but Magoo was one of a kind.

I had never flown in a chopper before, so when the producer told me I was getting the chance to go up for a quick flight, I was over the moon. When Magoo walked into the camp to introduce himself, he was wearing his ripped ringer shirt, shorts, and no shoes, and had a six-pack of Great Northern tucked under his arm. He was totally unmissable, a big man with a big smile—someone you would want on your side if a bar fight broke out.

I made a joke about his bare feet. I asked him when the last time he wore shoes was and he said he couldn't really remember—maybe five years ago. I thought he was joking, but he wasn't. The bottom of his feet had a layer of skin so thick he might as well have been wearing thongs; I imagined it would feel about the same.

He truly was the quintessential barefoot bush pilot, the ones who learned in the bush and stayed in the bush, spending days mustering cattle, doing remote station work, putting out fires, and everything in between. Magoo was quite remarkable: he hadn't grown up in a life of luxury and he didn't learn how to read or write until he had to pass the theory component of his helicopter license. His flying skills were immaculate, and I asked him if he had ever crashed. I was expecting maybe a faulty landing story, not expecting the wild tale he told me next.

He had been flying over the ocean in his youth when he had an engine failure—not ideal. His chopper came crashing down and hit the water; when he came to consciousness, he was strapped tight by his seatbelt at the bottom of the ocean. He needed oxygen fast, so he tore free of the seatbelt and swam to the surface. Miraculously, a fishing boat had seen the crash and came over to save him. Magoo must have had a guardian angel looking out for him that day; he left the crash with just a few broken ribs. To this day, it's one of those stories that no one believes, but Magoo and the other locals swear black and blue it happened.

After we wrapped up filming in the Palmer we set off to Cooktown, a small town in FNQ on the ocean. Magoo took the three boys and me in the chopper so we didn't have to do the four-hour drive through the ranges and rivers. The chopper had no doors, and the views were insane. The parts of Australia that are the most untouched and least visited are the most spectacular. We flew over gorges, massive steep hills, mangroves, and terrain that transformed from dry and rough to tropical and green. We flew following the river to its mouth, and when the river opened into the ocean my jaw dropped. The crystal-blue water meeting the rust-red dirt is an incredibly unique contrast that makes me proud to be from this beautiful country. It was the middle of summer and we all wanted nothing more than to swim in the clear warm ocean—but unfortunately it's full of sharks, crocodiles, and Irukandji jellyfish, so it wasn't worth the risk.

We got to fly through Hells Gate, though, and Magoo told us all about its history. In the original gold rush, prospectors in the Palmer faced starvation during the wet season; rising rivers meant they were stuck without supplies. As a result, five Aboriginal troopers and a sub inspector had to blaze a new track between the goldfields and Cooktown, which was 140 kilometers away, to ensure the prospectors didn't die. The track was only suitable for travel by foot and horseback, as there was a narrow opening between two huge boulders at the top of the escarpment that a cart couldn't fit through. This opening became a notorious spot for ambushes and as a result came to be called Hells Gate. Many people lost their lives there. I guess that happens when you try to colonize civilizations that have been living there for over 60,000 years.

The track was remarkable to see from the sky. It was long and rough, and I couldn't imagine walking the 140 kilometers in the heat and humidity, constantly fearing an ambush. We could also see little patches of fruit trees growing where old-timers set up stores along the way. Magoo pointed out places where breweries, orchards, and post offices were set up. We then followed another river and got so close to the banks we could see huge saltwater crocodiles sunbaking on the sand. We followed it all the way to Cooktown.

Cooktown is a small, remote country town, but FNQ style: the locals were friendly, but all of them carried some wild stories. The town had a small supermarket, a hotel, a great health food store, and some other local businesses. We spent the two nights we had there at the local pub, as you do when you're coming out of a week in the bush.

Everyone was betting at the TAB and drinking XXXX, and we were chatting to the locals. I asked one what he did for work, and noticed it seemed to be common that they worked in the fishing industry. I got chatting to a couple of fishermen who free dived for crays in the area, which blew my mind. You must be a certain kind of hard to free dive in the waters off FNQ.

I asked them if they feared sharks and crocs, and they both replied in sync, "Ah, nup." One of the guys told me he once had a croc and a bull shark follow him on the same day. I was dumbfounded.

What kind of crazy do you have to be to think that's enjoyable? And considering some of the times I've had with my bipolar, *me* calling someone crazy is really saying something.

One of the leases we tested in FNQ had a caretaker, an old Serbian man living out in the bush there. He lived in a little shack next to the river, hours from civilization. This guy never wore a shirt, barely spoke English, and lived off gold. We rocked up to the lease quite late, so we ended up camping on the riverbed next to his shack.

It was a beautiful area. We caught yabbies and cooked them on the fire, drank some beers, told some stories, and slept open-top in our swags. The river homed some freshwater crocs, but the caretaker assured us that they wouldn't hurt us; he'd shoot them and eat them for dinner sometimes. I was so content; it was one of those nights that made me realize just how lucky I am to live this life.

The next day, I needed to do some testing with our little wet plant to see how the ground was. Obviously, it's vital to find gold before buying a gold lease. It wasn't until that moment that I realized that the type of lease didn't permit prospecting with mechanical means, which is very standard throughout Australia. You need to have certain permits in place before you can just start digging up the countryside; it's the government's way of regulating the mining and prospecting industry.

I'd wrongly assumed they would have these permits ready to go for us; our wet plant was mechanical. I'd had one job and managed to majorly fuck it up. I was extremely embarrassed—I had dragged Parker and the whole film crew out to the middle of nowhere for a lease that we couldn't even test. It was the first time I received a "you need to be better" talk from Parker and it was a massive wake-up call. It stung coming from him because I was always worried our professional relationship would impact our personal relationship. It needed to be the one and only mistake I'd make. Not only had I disappointed Parker and wasted money and resources, but I had also embarrassed myself on international television and risked my business reputation. It was also a horrific comparison to Victoria and a very bad start to my stupid promise that we'd find better, which I was regretting with every inch of my body. I didn't say that, though. I backed myself and swallowed my pride.

I was clearly a bit irritated with myself and that's when George, the Serbian caretaker, shouted in his broken English, "Ahhhhh, fuck the fucking mines department! Test it anyway. Who cares about their dumb rules." It was a highly illegal suggestion and a bit hard to hide when it would have been aired on a massive TV show. I thought he was joking, but he wasn't; he really did not care at all. He told me that they would never find him because he was so remote. The Palmer was such a difficult place to get to that it would have been extremely hard for them to monitor everything happening there. It gets rain for months during the wet season, and during the dry season the hills are so steep and the roads so rough that it is still extremely hard to get in and out at the best of times. If you don't want to be found, it's the perfect place to be.

One of the guys in the pub laughed when I told him about George; he said that it was very PG for what really goes down out there. He told me about all the times he had been shot at for being on someone else's lease and how he had been run down by angry prospectors. He'd even lost a mate out there to gold fever.

He and his best friend were prospecting out in a remote part of FNQ. They'd had the same agreement for ten years: you split everything you find, fifty-fifty, always. One year, they were having a tough time; it was coming close to the end of their season and they were nowhere near their target. He noticed his friend was acting a little irritable, but he didn't think much of it.

On the second-last day they hit a patch—a big patch. They were pulling out nuggets left, right, and center. I could imagine their relief as he was speaking. So many palm-sized nuggets were coming out of the ground that they couldn't keep up. It was a prospector's dream: the lotto win that makes all the losing tickets worth it.

The biggest nugget they pulled was a 10-ouncer, which is a great find. They were both ecstatic, over the moon. As a prospector, I know that feeling so well: you've been on the baked beans for so long, the stress is building, and the job you once loved is turning into a nightmare. You're barely finding enough gold to pay fuel and food, you're beginning to question your abilities and life choices, and then—bam—you hit the lobster, finally, and you remember again why you do what you do. They had finally found their lobster and they were on top of the world.

To celebrate, they opened a bottle of Jack and sat by the fire drinking, singing, and being merry. They had pulled a 100-ounce patch that would keep their lifestyle going, and life was truly great. He went to sleep that night knowing he was taking home enough gold to support his family through the off season, and every ounce of stress had vanished.

When 2 a.m. hit, though, he woke from his dreams to a full-blown nightmare: his best friend holding a gun to his head, screaming, "Get up! Get up! Get up!" He pleaded with his friend, but knew exactly what was about to happen: his best mate of ten years was holding him at gunpoint to take the gold. He had it all in his caravan for them to split back in town, as usual, but his best mate had caught gold fever and wanted it all for himself. This man handed the gold over and begged again with his friend, but his pleas were falling on deaf ears. He lost $125,000, a best friend, and his love for the game all within ten minutes.

The friend took off, never to be seen again. It's a story I have heard over and over. The characters change but the plot doesn't. I asked him why he didn't go to the police, but I knew why, and he gave me a look that confirmed my suspicions. It's very common in the gold game to bend the rules or avoid them altogether—especially in a place like the Palmer or remote parts of Western Australia and the Northern Territory.

The gold world is a massive grey area. Gold is not trackable. It's worth its weight in, well, gold, and is extremely easy to mine, buy, and sell with no trace. I could find a $10,000 nugget and have it sold within a week without paying tax or letting the government know about its very existence. The gold world was lawless for a very long time and the prospectors that are around today were born into that lawless world. It may be more regulated now, but they all know exactly how to avoid the modern rules.

I'd put money on that man in the pub keeping the story from police because the patch they'd found was ground they weren't allowed on. Alternatively, he might have had illegal processing methods in his home, owned illegal processing chemicals, or avoided tax—or a mixture of these things.

You do not want to raise any red flags when you're a gold

prospector who isn't playing by the rules. Flying under the radar is the only way to survive. So he copped it on the chin and learned a rule many other prospectors have also learned the hard way: you're better off alone.

I went for breakfast at the hotel the next day and the waitress asked where I had come in from and I told her the Palmer. She responded instantly with "Oh God, it's filled with crazy people, and it's haunted as hell."

I normally wouldn't think much of the haunted comment—a lot of old mining areas are said to be haunted, and although I believe in spirits, it's usually just hyperbole—but my ears pricked up because I'd had the weirdest experience two days earlier while I was running through the Palmer ranges.

I had decided to go for a jog by myself after we had finished filming for the day, just before sunset. I was half an hour in and running through the bush when I decided to follow a sign left toward an old townsite. Midrun, I heard my name being called. I froze and looked around; I was in the middle of nowhere and there was no one to be seen. Shivers went down my spine and I had an overwhelming feeling that I was being watched.

I kept running and told myself it was nothing, when I began to hear something coming from down the creek. It was chatting and laughing, clear as day. I was literally in the middle of nowhere, far from any roads. Every inch of my body was telling me to get out, so I turned around and ran home. I told everyone what happened, but they shrugged it off and no one really believed me.

It didn't seem like much, but it's not the first time that has happened to me. I have many stories of hearing my name being shouted out, my parents hearing giggling at night, unexplained laughter coming from behind our camp, a random but deep sense of being watched when prospecting. Most prospectors or people who spend time out in the bush will have similar experiences. You can also speak to any Indigenous person, and they will tell you of spirits in the bush that you don't mess with. No matter what it was, it was something, and it's another reason to be careful out in the outback.

By the end of our time in FNQ, the fun and excitement that Parker and I were keeping behind closed doors inevitably began to seep out. Our coworkers were growing suspicious, and the "we're just friends" game was getting a little old. When we hit Cairns, Parker confided in Danny, and, without Parker's knowledge, I confided in a fellow Australian crew member (most of the crew was from the UK). The secret was weighing on me, and I needed to share that weight with a friend. I don't think either Danny or that crew member were completely shocked, but both were impressed at our sneaking-about skills. I was glad we had concealed it well; it was important to me that my onscreen relationship with Parker was portrayed as nothing but professional to ensure my position on the show wasn't questioned. I wanted people to know I was there for my skill—and nothing else.

13

GOD'S COUNTRY

Halls Creek, better known as Hells Crack, is one hell of a town and was the next stop on our trip. One night there will give you a clear indication as to why it's named after the doorway to the devil. Flies, heat, isolation, lack of resources, heat, flash flooding, bush fires, deadly animals, heat, drought, the wet season, the build-up to the wet season, crime, systemic racism, and the heat are just some of the reasons the town has earned its name.

I have been to Halls Creek on a couple of occasions. It's in the Kimberley, God's country, and has a community feel that I personally love—but it is an extremely hard place to survive in. The first time I visited Hells Crack was to film *Aussie Gold Hunters* and I ended up having my twenty-third birthday there. The second time I visited was to film *Parker's Trail*.

Both visits were at the worst time of year: the build-up to the wet season. The build-up on the top half of Australia is extremely muggy—100 percent humidity paired with 100-degree days—so you basically spend the day bathing in your own sweat.

I feel a connection to Hells Crack even though it's given me a lot of reasons not to. I have been stuck in extreme flash flooding, outrun wild bushfires, and even been robbed there (more on that later), but my favorite story is one of heroism and bravery, two traits that highlight the good side of small remote communities like this one.

Old Halls Creek is 15 kilometers away from the new town site. Nothing much remains there except some ruins of the original town, an abandoned caravan park, and an old gravesite. The gravesite has over 200 marked and unmarked graves from the original gold rush, which only lasted three months in Old Halls Creek because extreme conditions meant the prospectors were dropping like flies. The gravesite has also listed some of the names and ages of the people buried there, and they range from infants to people in their early thirties.

As you walk in through the gates, on your immediate left is an old gravestone marked James "Jimmy" Darcy. It's one of the bigger ones in the cemetery; the people who were given these were always from a wealthy background or respected in the community. The stone is engraved with: 'The memory of James Darcy, who died at Halls Creek 22nd of August 1917 aged 29 years. RIP'. He was only a couple years older than I am, and little did he know his story would change life for Australians in the outback forever. Jimmy's death ignited a national debate about the lack of medical services in the outback, and the ensuing butterfly effect is the reason I can prospect full-time in the outback, knowing help is only a phone call away if I truly need it.

Jimmy was a stockman, and had a bad fall off a horse 50 kilometers out of Halls Creek, really the definition of bum fuck nowhere. He was carted into town hoping to find a doctor, but was instead met by the postmaster, the only person there who had a little bit of first aid training. Using morse code, the postmaster communicated with Dr. Holland, who was hundreds of kilometers away in Perth. The doctor encouraged the postmaster to attempt surgery, and when the postmaster fretted that he'd accidentally kill Jimmy, the doctor replied, "He will die anyway."

So, unbelievably, they strapped Jimmy down in the post office, used alcohol as a disinfectant (and a painkiller, I'm guessing), sharpened the kitchen utensils, and began operating on Jimmy's injuries. The postmaster communicated throughout the operation with the doctor in Perth, still using only morse code. I couldn't even order a bagel in morse code, let alone attempt to save someone's life. The operation was grueling and went for seven hours—seven very long hours—but it was a success. Or at least they thought.

Despite the operation seemingly going well, Jimmy was not improving; Dr. Holland made a mercy dash to Halls Creek. Perth to Halls Creek is not an easy trip today; 100 years ago, it was a long two weeks. Dr. Holland had to take a cattle boat to Derby, which took five days, and then two separate cars to travel the rest of the distance. The cars would break down constantly due to the horrible roads and bad conditions; Dr. Holland eventually had to ditch the second car to walk to a nearby cattle station, from which he made the final leg of the journey by horseback.

Before the last leg of the journey, Dr. Holland phoned the postmaster to check on Jimmy. He was in a bad way, but he was holding on. Dr. Holland then jumped in a Ford to drive the final five days to reach Halls Creek. Unfortunately, it was twenty-four hours too late; Jimmy had passed due to malaria the night before Dr. Holland arrived.

Jimmy's story was one of thousands in the early gold rush days, but it struck a chord with the right people. Lieutenant Clifford Peel, a young Victorian medical student and aviator, witnessed the heartache in the outback and wrote an extremely moving letter to the founder of the Australian Inland Mission, Reverend John Flynn, suggesting using aircrafts to transport medical relief to the outback. Unfortunately, Peel was shot down in combat over in France shortly after, and never got to see that his letter became the blueprint for the Royal Flying Doctor Service.

Flynn began a ten-year campaign to create an aerial medical service to act as a "mantle of support" for the outback. In 1928, eleven years after Jimmy's death, long-term supporter of the venture Hugh McKay left a huge sum of money to Flynn to make it a reality; today, we have the Royal Flying Doctor Service.

Just about every Australian understands the importance of the Royal Flying Doctor Service. For any Aussie living and working in the bush, it's the difference between surviving and not. For us, it is our lifeline. I am so lucky that I have only been present on one occasion when the Flying Doctor was called. A friend was prospecting on Yamaji land, about 170 kilometers from the closest nurse's post, when she had symptoms of a cancer relapse. She quickly deteriorated, and the Flying Doctor Service was urgently called. They were there quicker than the five-hour drive to a real hospital, landing on the closest road to airlift her to Kalgoorlie Hospital. The

Royal Flying Doctor Service saved her life that day.

Neither Flynn nor Peel ever got to see how many thousands of Australians they indirectly saved. There have been some great Aussies to come out of the outback, and these are two of them. For me, the outback brings out a humanity in people that is harder to find in the city. It's so unfortunate that gold fever can come along and taint that, but Flynn's and Peel's humanity still exists out in the bush even today.

As much as I loved exploring the beautiful Kimberleys, the reason we were there was to find a potential mining claim for Parker. I thank whoever is up in the sky looking after me for letting us enjoy such success at Palmer River before Halls Creek, because, Jesus Christ, leaving Victoria would have looked like the worst decision ever if we'd gone straight to Halls Creek.

Halls Creek has historically produced a lot of gold; quantity wasn't necessarily the problem. It was who we were potentially trying to buy the ground from—they weren't as easy to work with as my previous contacts. We were tired, and everything seemed to go wrong. It was extremely hard work: we had a mechanical breakdown at every corner, people soiling samples and barely any gold. It was bad enough that there was even talk about leaving early and not finishing the episode altogether. We were all exhausted and wanted out.

We had carted our wet plant thousands of kilometers around Australia by this point, including through a deep river crossing, and it was absolutely cooked. It was not even close to working. Hence why I really regret being a stinge and not buying the brand-new wash plant that was over budget. There were many of the "Well, if the wash plant wasn't old" comments thrown around, and Fred and I just copped it on the chin. We needed that wet plant up and running; we didn't have any other means to test the fines. It was the only option.

Fred and Danny were confident they could fix it, and with Parker and me hanging around, there were too many cooks in the kitchen. I could tell Parker was getting very irritated as well, so I decided to take him to a natural spring for a bit of a breather and to hopefully find some gold.

On top of everything else that was going wrong, concealing my relationship with Parker was becoming next to impossible. One night, in the sticky heat of the build-up, it all came to a head. Craig, our executive producer, was sleeping in a room right next to Parker's. So my sneaking skills had to be stepped up a notch. It was tradition after a long, hot day of filming to spend the evening at the pub, drinking beer and playing pool. This night was no different. We had a game or three of pool, nursed several beers in the warm Kimberley weather, laughed with the locals at Halls Creek's favorite watering hole, and then went to bed. This was, of course, followed by me waiting for the coast to be clear before making the 40-meter dash to Parker's room.

The next morning, we all woke up and made our way down to the dining room as usual for breakfast and coffee together. Danny and Fred then began a slightly bizarre conversation: they were both woken up during the night by knocks on their door, which was weird. I was barely listening to them as I ate my toasted sandwich, thinking about working in the 113-degree heat that day. Before we all jumped in the car for the thirty-minute desert drive to the gold mine we were visiting, I raced back to my room to find my backpack, which I never left behind. I couldn't find it, though, and I could have sworn I'd left it in my room. We were already running late, though, so I went without it and didn't think much of it, assuming I had misplaced it somewhere. When we got back at lunch, I went to the pub to see if I had left it there, hoping it would be waiting behind the bar for me. It wasn't. I searched Parker's room, our truck, and all the other camera crew cars.

By this stage, I was starting to get a little nervous. We had been traveling to all of these great gold mines around Australia, and at almost every stop along the way, miners and prospectors had given us pieces of gold to keep. We never got to keep the gold we helped find or watched the miners find—it was their ground and their gold— but most of the miners were nice enough to give us a couple of little nuggets as keepsakes. We were planning to split them among us all at the end; I thought it would be a nice gesture, a piece of Australia for each crew member to have. I stored all of that gold, as well as a wallet full of cash, my cards, my passport, and my laptop, in my backpack— the backpack I couldn't find. My stomach dropped when I realized that my laptop, cards, and passport had all been stacked on top of my bed when I'd checked it before work. It was like I had taken them out of my backpack and placed them there, but I had no memory of doing that. Then it clicked.

"I think I was robbed last night!" I blurted out loud to Danny.

"What do you mean, "robbed"?" He replied. "Someone came in your room when you were sleeping?"

"Well, yes," I said. "Where else would my bag be!"

No one believed me and they were certain I had still lost it, "it" being the bag or the plot. Still, I just knew I had been robbed. We were in Hells Crack, after all. Confident in my accusations, I went to the front desk and asked security to check the cameras. They watched back, and, sure enough, two men had climbed the fence, scoured the premises, and were seen walking toward my bedroom.

The knocks on Danny's and Fred's rooms suddenly made sense: the thieves were checking for sounds inside the rooms. When my room was knocked on, there was of course dead silence. It had only been a matter of time before sleeping with a coworker would have some consequences, although I hadn't expected that being robbed would be one of them.

The realization of what that meant then hit me—my money was gone, yes, but more importantly so was all of our gold. I had to explain this to the guys, and I felt so bad. The thieves weren't only clever, but lucky too. Gold really is the perfect thing to steal; from the start of the goldrush until now gold theft is hard to track and hard to prove. There aren't receipts for gold nuggets, and gold only takes ten minutes to melt down and thus remove any serial numbers. It's nearly untraceable in smaller amounts, and extremely easy to sell no matter where you are in the world—even in the middle of the desert, you can move smaller amounts within twenty-four hours. The irony doesn't escape me that after my ancestor's role in dealing stolen gold, I was now on the receiving end. Gold is greed dressed in a pretty coat. Where there is gold, there will always be crime.

I am very appreciative that they went to the effort of leaving my passport, laptop, and laptop charger on my bed, though. I'd like to say it was very thoughtful, but laptops are hard to move in the desert, and trackable, so they aren't worth the effort.

Within the hour, the police arrived to take my report. They confirmed to me that it would be hard to get the gold and cash back, but they would try. They also looked at my window and showed me how the robbers had got in; they had simply taken out the window fixings and climbed through, which was quite unsettling and proved the accommodation's security wasn't as good as I had initially thought. I am so glad I wasn't in the room when that happened, but it still added to my feeling of never being fully relaxed, even in the remote outback.

Once the police left, I walked over to the crew. This included the two producers, the director and Parker, who were discussing our next scene. We chatted about how unlucky it was, and how we all had to be extra vigilant with the expensive kit the crew had. I wanted to reply with "No shit, I've been saying this for weeks," but decided to just agree. All of a sudden, Craig, the big boss, swiftly turned to me from across the group, tilted his head to the left, and gave me a very knowing look. I knew exactly what was about to come out of his mouth, but stupidly had not prepared an intelligent, well-thought-out response.

"Tyler," he said. "What time did this happen?"

The whole group turned and looked at me.

"Three a.m.," I muttered. That was when the penny dropped; everyone in the group knew exactly where Craig was going with this.

His eyebrows raised, and my stomach dropped: "Tyler, where were you if you weren't in your room at three am?"

I froze. Everyone was dead silent, and for once I didn't have any words. Sheena, one of my friends and a producer, jumped in to have my back: "She was with me." It would have been believable if both Parker and I weren't standing there, awkwardly glaring at each other, hoping the other person would have a good explanation. As it was, Craig smirked and said, "What you both do in your alone time is none of my business," and that was the end of that.

After Halls Creek, we spent one night in Broome as a break—a much needed break. Finally, we got to see the ocean after spending weeks on end in the desert. Unfortunately, it was during the build-up, so, due to the two types of deadly jellyfish hanging around, we couldn't swim on beautiful Cable Beach. There was also a saltwater crocodile sighting a couple of days earlier. Good old Australia: beautiful at first glance, but will kill you if you look at it the wrong way!

We spent the night smoking and drinking at the open-air cinemas and got some rest before heading back into the desert. By this time, we had hit the Murchison in the middle of summer—a time when I had to repeatedly remind myself, "I love my job, I love my job, I love my job."

I spent my twenty-fourth birthday in a town called Yalgoo, where we filmed a prospector and his hard-rock mine. No offense to the town of Yalgoo, but it is probably one of the last places in Australia I would have chosen to spend a birthday. It was beyond lucky that by this point the boys and the film crew were my family, which made it one of my favorite birthdays to date.

Yalgoo consists of a pub, a petrol station, and a fuckload of flies. The pub wasn't even open on my birthday—but luckily the pub owner was a legend and opened the bar for us to have some drinks and play some pool. Parker bought everyone a round of shots to celebrate, and Brad, the producer, gave me a speech. I have a photo of the boys and me drinking rum while sitting on the pool table, and it reminds me of how content I was. It was one of the first times I had felt true happiness in a long time.

Kalgoorlie, my home town, was the last stop before we were done. After three months of hard work, I was so excited to show everyone where I was from. I had spent such a long time in unfamiliar gold country, basically winging a lot of it, and finally we were in my stomping ground. I felt so much more confident, and I was so excited to show everyone my prospecting skills in my backyard.

We found good gold, and Parker even found a lease that he liked, so we pegged it. A big win in my eyes. Even though we had the Palmer as a viable mining operation, the Kalgoorlie lease was another great option. It was extremely different from what Parker was used to, so I felt accomplished getting to teach him new techniques and show him how my family and I did things.

Any prospector will tell you the troubles they have with claim jumpers or gold poachers—my family and I have a million stories. They are everywhere. Another slight mistake due to a lack of communication between Parker and me meant that claim jumpers were detecting on Parker's new lease.

Parker caught them, and after a small chase and a lot of confusion, I had to explain to him that the "claim jumpers" weren't doing anything wrong. Unlike in the Yukon, in Western Australia once a lease is pegged it goes into a pending state for eight to twelve months while the paperwork goes through. During this pending stage, the ground is free for anyone to prospect on. So the claim jumpers were legally allowed to be there and in fact Parker could have got in some heat for attempting to chase them off. I assumed Parker knew about the pending stage, but as my dad always says—to assume makes an ass out of u and me.

While Parker was irritated, he luckily understood how the confusion came in, though it did put a dampener on the Kalgoorlie lease. The pending stage also means mining cannot commence until it's approved, which meant it wasn't mineable for up to another year. That would have been fine, but cue the global pandemic. COVID would crush that dream.

After Kalgoorlie, we hit Perth. Production put us up in a huge house in the Perth hills with a pool overlooking the valley. After three months in the desert traveling in a HiLux, living on top of one another, and searching for gold, this was absolute bliss. We filmed the final episode and had an amazing wrap party right on the beach in Scarborough.

On the one hand, I was so happy to be back in civilization, drinking cocktails on the beach; on the other, reality had sunk in. Our journey was over, and my new family was about to fly back home to the other side of the world and Parker and I would have to go our separate ways. It was hard for me to say goodbye to everyone. We had been through many ups and downs together, and even though it was work, I really did consider them to be family.

I'd especially become so close with the three boys; Parker, Danny and Fred, and they had come into my life at a time when I really needed them. Without them even realizing, that job and those people played a huge role in my mental health recovery. Not only had

I just come out of a seven-year relationship and a massive depressive episode, but I was also at a crossroads in my life. That job took me down a path of hope, fulfillment, and success. I think if the universe hadn't opened that door for me, the other path would have looked a lot darker.

Danny and I planned to go see Flume in London together, Fred and I made a million plans to hang out in the US, and Parker invited me to spend some time with him and his family in Alaska with no plans to end the relationship we had started. Parker and I left off on such a good note that I was feeling very positive about our future. These plans made it so much easier to say goodbye because I knew it wasn't forever. I am so glad that I, along with the rest of the world, was so naive about how 2020 would go down and how many plans, big and small, would never play out.

I was lucky enough to visit Parker at the start of 2020, just before the shitshow of the pandemic began. I flew into Vancouver and spent a couple of days exploring the city with Parker before we traveled to Vancouver Island. Vancouver Island was such a highlight for me. Its scenery is breathtaking, the complete opposite from my backyard of red dirt.

We partied with some of Parker's friends while on the island, and I stumbled back with some of them to the Empress Hotel, a very expensive and fancy hotel we were staying at. One theme from my younger years is that I'd take the partying and drinking a little too far. It's one thing I am constantly trying to improve on, but at that point hadn't quite mastered; for some reason I still can't explain, I thought it would be funny to set off the hotel's fire alarm at 3 a.m.

It was not funny. The whole hotel was evacuated, and the

fire brigade showed up. Once I came to my senses, I cried to the receptionist, explaining how sorry I was. She looked at me and said, "Stop crying, get back in the line, and act like it wasn't you. Trust me, it's better that way." That receptionist saved me a huge fine and potential jail time that night, and I learned a very valuable lesson: your drunk ideas are nowhere near as funny as you think they are.

It was on my way back from Canada that COVID started to come in thick. I didn't really understand the severity of it; I don't think anyone did. I made it back into Australia just as the world began to lock down.

At this point, I realized that I didn't know when I would see Parker again. Long distance is hard, especially when you're both in the middle of a pandemic with no plans to see each other and are unsure about what is going on. I often felt anxious about how it would play out; I need a lot of communication in relationships to feel secure, and, due to the circumstances, ours didn't have enough. To add to the mix, I would receive hundreds of messages, articles, and videos every week from people desperate to know if Parker and I were an item. I hated the fact that people were more interested in my dating life than my career or me as a person, but I understood it. The *Gold Rush* audience loved Parker; they had watched him grow up and wanted him to be happy. They weren't just invested in the gold, they were invested in him as a person, as you would be with a friend. I was extremely cautious of using Parker to gain fame and opportunities. I never wanted to post about our personal relationship because I didn't want him to think I was using him for personal gain. I also didn't want the audience to think my spot on the show, or any of my future achievements, were thanks to our relationship. The possibility of them questioning my abilities made me very worried.

After returning to Australia, I moved my life back from Perth to Kalgoorlie and finally gave up work in the hospitality industry. I tried to hold on to the fact that if my relationship with Parker was meant to be, it would be—and, after a while, I started to realize that maybe it wasn't. It was a hard pill to swallow, but when I got the news that *Parker's Trail* wasn't going ahead in 2020 due to COVID, any last chance of us seeing each other disappeared and there wasn't much point holding on. After six or so months our communication dried up. Though I hoped our working relationship wasn't over, I knew romantically it was. Sure enough, after some Instagram sleuthing (which we're all guilty of, aren't we? No? Maybe just me?) I found out he was dating someone else. Thankfully for my mental health, it came at a time when I had healed from that part of my life; I was happy for him, and all that mattered to me was that he was in a good place.

That's when it hit me, though—this could impact my career. It was a moment I hadn't thought about, a possible consequence I hadn't acknowledged. I had been warned of this, but I just always assumed he wouldn't let what happened between us impact our professional relationship. Was I incredibly naive? At the end of the day, it was his show, and if he or his girlfriend didn't want me around, then I would be dropped in a heartbeat. Being liked by the audience didn't hold much merit in this situation; it was *Parker's Trail*, not *Tyler's Trail*. If Parker wanted to replace me, it would be an extremely easy feat. I reminded myself that if it was meant to be, it would be—and if he decided I wasn't on the show anymore, I would be okay.

I went back to full-time prospecting and was single for the first time since seventeen. It was the beginning of my new life and my year of crossroads, ups, downs, lessons, and blessings. The year 2020 began with a global pandemic, and ended with a hospitalization, a book deal, and a completely new version of myself.

Traveling Australia, working in the gold game, and growing up in the outback, I saw firsthand how gender inequality plays out in the workplace. In my case, I became used to my looks always being rated and praised before my skill.

It makes it hard to be taken seriously when people consider "beautiful" women to be objects, not humans. You can't possibly be pretty *and* smart, can you? I can see it in men's eyes when I tell them that I am a successful business owner: "What? *You* run a business?" I know my age has something to do with it, but I can see their brain wigging out, trying to process that someone they have identified as pretty is also smart. It's not a narrative that is considered normal in the patriarchy.

I can also see it when I google my name. After four seasons on television as a gold miner and prospector, years of running a successful gold prospecting business, and creating a mental health podcast, the first five headlines are always about my relationship status and if Parker and I are dating.

If you google Fred Lewis, my male peer, his first five headlines are about his career journey and how much gold he is finding. It's so hard for women to get a seat at the table, and when we finally do, like landing a job on *Gold Rush*, we aren't taken anywhere near as seriously as our male counterparts.

The difference in media coverage shows that Fred's career is taken more seriously than mine; the media would rather discuss my dating life than my career success, prospecting skills, and business moves. In YouTube videos I am called hot, while Parker is called a great miner. How can women be taken seriously and given the same opportunities if our bodies and dating life are considered more important than our skills?

Pretty privilege is something that has always interested me: the idea that people who fit the Western standards of beauty are given extra privileges in life. Beauty is subjective, but a small nose, white skin, blond hair, clear skin, curves in the "right" places, and a lean body are all characteristics that fit Western beauty standards. There is no denying that women who are seen as beautiful are treated extremely differently from those who aren't.

I know a lot of opportunities that have been given to me are due to my looks. If you read any comment section on a *Gold Rush* article, you'll see that I receive a lot of positive feedback—not about my skills, but about my appearance: "We love Tyler, she's pretty," "get Tyler back, she is easy on the eyes," and "Tyler did a great job—she is good to look at." There is another woman on the main *Gold Rush* show who doesn't fit these beauty standards, and the comments about her are disgusting—again, nothing to do with her skill level but her looks. I would love to be able to do my job and only be judged on my ability. Why can't they comment on my prospecting skills and not the color of my eyes? It's hard for me, and know I have it much easier than women who don't fit the bill. This is why I find it a little short-sighted when I see successful, "pretty" white women state that it's not luck that got them to where they are, but in fact hard work.

I get it, of course. The statement "you're so lucky" is invalidating to all the hard work you put into your success, especially when there is no denying that you worked your arse off. Especially in a patriarchy, I praise any woman for success in any form, not just the usual definition. It's hard fucking work—*but* I also think it's very irresponsible to not acknowledge the part pretty privilege plays in said successes. I have no idea how many doors were opened for me due to my race, class, and looks; the best I can do is acknowledge that it wasn't just hard work that helped me be successful. There is also a lot of luck and privilege involved.

Pretty privilege does give us attention and it does open doors, but it isn't always the attention we want and it also can close the doors we need. It comes with a whole range of negative consequences. I am careful when I say this because I don't want it to come across as, "Oh, poor pretty people, getting too much attention." I say it to bring light to the fact that this attention, when it comes from men, is mostly coming from a place of objectification and misogyny.

There have been countless times that I wanted to cut off all my hair, strap down my boobs, and wear baggy clothes so I could leave the house without men staring. It's a feeling a lot of women experience; pretty privilege may get you a free drink at the bar, but it also gets you catcalled on the way home. Catcalling may seem like a compliment to some but it can be paralyzing, especially to women who have experienced prior sexual harassment. I was first catcalled when I was twelve. The yelling out the window doesn't make me feel good, it makes me feel unsafe. It makes me feel like the people who I know can hurt me are watching me and noticing me. It's very intimidating; I would give up my pretty privilege if it meant no man would notice me—ever. Maybe then I would be able to walk alone at night without being terrified I'll be the next rape victim.

With this being said, women who use their pretty privilege to get in front are often punished; under the patriarchy, we are taught that women who cover up deserve more respect than those who don't. Rape culture has us victim blaming and too often asking questions like "what was she wearing?" or "well, wasn't she dressed slutty?" or "what did she expect in shorts like that?" My friend was sexually assaulted when she was nine. She was wearing Playschool pajamas. At the end of the day, it's not the outfit that gets us raped—it's rapists. Women should be able to live without fear that their outfits will incite stares, whistles, or assault. This will happen when women are seen as humans, not objects.

Telling women on social media to "put their clothes back on and be respectful" when they post a photo in swimwear or a dress is a part of rape culture. An outfit or our appearance has nothing to do with the level of respect we deserve, and pushing an agenda saying otherwise proves the narrative that only men can decide if a woman deserves to be respected.

The shame doesn't stop at clothes and bodies, either. Women are often shamed for getting Botox or fillers because we are only allowed to be beautiful if it's natural. In a world where we are told from the earliest stages of childhood that a woman's looks determine their worth, where we are told wrinkles are disgusting, where we are told that to be loved you must be conventionally beautiful, having cosmetic work done can feel like an act of survival.

If I must get Botox under my eyes to help me love myself, I will; you can't blame a woman for doing that when we have this narrative shoved down our throats every second of the day. You do what you must to survive the patriarchy; don't let anyone tell you otherwise. Natural is not best, self-love is best. Plastic is not fake, but beauty is beauty. I am not less for having work done.

On the trip for *Parker's Trail*, I met up with a friend who also worked in mining. She explained to me that she was going to quit because of the unfair treatment her male supervisor was giving her compared to her male colleagues. This is very typical for any women working in a male-dominated field, and I've grown up right in the pits of it. I asked her if she explained to her boss that she was leaving because of her misogynistic supervisor and she said yes, she did, and he replied, "There haven't been any outwardly nasty, mean, or misogynistic comments. If he had said out loud that he hates women then I could do something, but he didn't, so there's nothing I can do."

This is how it was handled even though she went through months of unfair treatment, and it is all too typical. It's a big reason a lot of women find it easier to keep their mouths shut. She then spoke to a woman who was high up in the mine and was told, "I know the feeling. There are so many bad pockets in the mining industry, but you just have to find the good ones." I disagree with this; I think we should remove the bad pockets and make all areas of the workforce a safe place for women.

These types of conversations and personal experiences once made me want to distance myself from the mining world. When I moved to Melbourne, it was so refreshing to be surrounded by men who weren't acting like it was the 1950s. I still had bad experiences with misogyny when I worked in the bar—unfortunately it's something we all deal with as women—but it was nothing compared to working in such potently male-dominated industries like mining and prospecting.

The patriarchal ideas that are so deeply rooted in the gold world are honestly exhausting. In the past I thought it was too much of a problem for me to take on; it was easier to stay away from it. As I have got older, my confidence and sense of self-worth have grown, and my attitudes have completely shifted. I want to be a part of the change; I want young girls to back themselves in a man's world, to see firsthand that it's possible to succeed in a male-dominated industry and that they should never back down because of their gender. I would rather it be me dealing with the crap from men in the industry than someone who isn't as confident in themselves. It may not seem like a lot, but if I can change the perspective of one man, or show a young girl that she can stand up for herself and follow the career she wants, then I will feel accomplished.

For the industry, the first step to remedying this culture is listening to women and believing them. Once I told my ex that I was too scared to go to the gas station at 10 p.m., and asked if he could come. I was worried because I had been catcalled at that gas station a couple of times. He replied, "You'll be fine," and with that one line completely invalidated all my experiences. It's hard enough living these moments, let alone having to constantly prove them to the people around you.

Working in the industry, I have also met many good men who

want to be better and make change; I feel very grateful to have been surrounded by allies like my dad and all of the boys and crew I met on *Parker's Trail*. The producers on the show—Craig, Carter, and Brad—were all extremely respectful and they always treated the women as equals.

Along the way, I've met many men who have made life easier for the women in their company. It's refreshing to not have to prove yourself all the time just because you're a woman. The problem definitely is not all men—but every woman has a story, which means that all men need to be a part of the solution.

After returning to Perth from *Parker's Trail*, empowered by the experience, I had a much clearer vision about what path I wanted to take. I wanted to be immersed in the gold world again, and running my own business. I was completely done with working for someone else and was committed to becoming a role model in the gold industry. I couldn't do that if I wasn't fully involved in it. I also fell back in love with gold prospecting—and being on those TV shows made me realize the rest of the world was falling as well.

I wanted to share our family's amazing knowledge with everyone else while preserving it along the way.

14

THE MOTHER LODE

In 2021, I began full-time prospecting with Mum, Dad, and Reece as well as running The Prospectors Club, and it was amazing. Nine years after leaving high school, I was finally doing what I loved and making money from it—not to mention working for myself.

If you asked Dad, he would joke and say he was my boss. While Mum and Dad technically had the final say in things, I had so much freedom, which is what I'd always been after. I could work on my business when I wanted, travel when I needed to, and I didn't have to cover my shift if I was sick. Prospecting gave me the lifestyle I'd always wanted, even though I'd spent years trying to run away from it.

It was great to be working with my family and very special to be working alongside my brother. When he left high school, he started working with Mum and Dad right away as a full-time prospector. Reece and I are like chalk and cheese: I am extroverted, he is introverted; I am loud, he is quiet; I love going out and he is a homebody. Despite our differences, we both share a passion for gold prospecting. It's been nice to grow and learn with him, and he has taught me a lot. We are both extremely stubborn and don't back down, but we also really complement each other. He is the digger operator and I am the loader operator. He loves working the scrapes with his detector and I love wandering with mine. He loves watching and researching upcoming tenements and I am good at the legalities. We are definitely a strong team.

Although I was finally feeling some fulfillment in my career, my mental health was still so up and down. I wasn't taking my diagnosis as seriously as I should have been, and this had catastrophic consequences for me and the people around me. One of the turning points for me was when one of my best friends gave me some advice. When you are going through life's troubles, people throw advice at you all day every day, but this one sentence helped shift my perspective forever—it's one of the reasons I have been able to see how important I am, just as me. My friend Lucy told me, "Tyler, when you walk into the room you light it up for a million reasons—and not one of those reasons is because you have a boyfriend."

That one sentence changed my outlook permanently. I could see that just me alone, with no partner, was enough and that I would be fine. Lucy has since passed and that was some of the last advice she gave me; she had this impact on everyone we met. It will be forever ingrained in my mind.

Lucy always had the most perfect thing to say in every situation. I first met her in Year 7 at primary school in Kalgoorlie, and even at that age the room always lit up when she walked in. She was funny, quick-witted, caring, thoughtful, and was always there whenever anyone needed her.

Not long after that, Lucy's health began to decline, and she eventually lost her battle with sarcoma. The grief of losing a best friend, someone you have known for fifteen years, and watching it rip apart every heart Lucy ever touched was something I had never experienced. Lucy's family are some of the most beautiful people you will ever meet and to see them in a world of pain was cruel. I have lost three grandparents to cancer, but this was so different. Watching someone so young and filled with so much light lose their battle made it hard to have faith in the universe.

Lucy's passing, the pandemic, my breakup, and moving back to Kalgoorlie all happened around the same time. Over the following months, I would stop seeing my psychologist, begin taking my lithium sporadically, start binge-drinking heavily, and enter six months of mania and hypomania—which ultimately ended with me in hospital.

As I've said before, mania and hypomania are euphoric, like being on a never-ending cocaine high—only it's not Saturday night in some bar, it's Tuesday lunchtime, and you are in the middle of a work meeting wondering why all your colleagues are asking you to slow down while you're halfway through booking flights to Mexico tomorrow morning with a credit card and also buying a microphone to start a podcast after lunch, while your colleague is annoying you because she is taking way too long to answer your question.

It's being on top of the world: everything is grandiose and splendid. I get filled with energy, I don't need sleep or food, and I have a million amazing, world-stopping ideas racing through my mind. Every idea I have is a great idea, and anyone who disagrees is wrong and trying to stop me from living my best life. I am freedom seeking, reckless, creative, impulsive, euphoric, and irritable all at the same time. I speak at a million miles an hour, drink more, and don't sleep, and I am searching for the next high. Everyone around me is moving too slowly and it's extremely irritating that they cannot keep up. Mania is like being on a roller-coaster ride that you can't get off, and everyone else is on the ground watching.

I always say that depression scares me a lot more than mania, but for the people who love me, mania is a whole lot scarier to watch. Sometimes you wouldn't even realize if I was having a depressive episode, but I might as well have carried around a flashing neon sign saying "I am a maniac" during 2020. For the people who barely knew me during this time in my life, they would have described me as "wild," "fun," "loud," and "intense," but my loved ones knew something more sinister was going on.

I began binge-drinking three to five nights a week—a good week was three nights, but often it would be more like four or five. I very often would run off two to three hours' sleep and be fine at work prospecting for gold. I would spend the day out bush with the detector, come home, and get ready to go again. I spent more time hungover and drunk than not. In my mind I was just having fun, though. I didn't see it as an issue because I was living my life and enjoying it.

While there is a lot of truth to that, it was also quite detrimental to my mental health. This all came to a head when I had a full-on manic episode over the Kalgoorlie Cup. Over five days, I had a total of ten hours' sleep and only ate one crumpet and one taco. Eating and sleeping patterns are huge indicators for a manic/depressive state; running off two hours' sleep for five days is not normal unless you're on drugs, but I wasn't doing enough of them to last that long. In this case, I only had a couple lines of cocaine and a shitload of alcohol—thanks, mania!

I had all the usual symptoms of an episode: excessive talking, no sleep, sexual promiscuity, substance abuse, irrationality, and impulsiveness. I was making decisions "normal" Tyler would never make; I got a life ban from the only club in town for doing cocaine on the dance floor, and in response I went home to change my outfit and redo my make-up so I could sneak back in.

My closest friends knew something was wrong. They didn't know what, but they knew I wasn't me. After this episode slowed about three weeks later, the inevitable happened and I reached rock bottom. It had been a long time coming; I'd spent years ignoring professional medical advice, avoiding my pills, and fighting my demons every single day while trying to ignore they were even there.

Even after my diagnosis, I didn't want to believe I was ill because I had such a privileged, perfect life. There was no "reason" for me to be sick. I am such a big believer in creating your own reality, so why was I choosing to create this for myself? *I am fine, my life is fine, this is just my personality,* I would tell myself about my manic episodes. It's hard when you are mentally ill, yet your brain tries to tell you you're making that mental illness up. The constant war in my brain over this while riding the depressions and manias of bipolar and dissociating from any resulting trauma finally caught up to me. I couldn't see a way out of how I was feeling, and I didn't want to do it anymore. I snapped.

It had been seven years of fighting my own mind, and the thought of living like that every single day until I died made me feel a sense of hopelessness I have never felt before. I couldn't see a light at the end of the tunnel. I didn't want to exist anymore. I just wanted to be gone and I couldn't control the intrusive thoughts that were just screaming at me to end it. After seven years of fighting, the demons had won and my mind had me pinned to the bottom of the ocean with no way out of its grip. I knew I would be missed, and I knew people would be sad, but I thought my life wasn't that important. Even if I was gone, the sun would still rise; the world would still turn. It would be hard, but everyone would be okay.

My impulsivity brings a lot of joy into my life sometimes, but that night it tried to end it all. I googled how much lithium it takes to overdose, then took that and then some more. I swallowed twenty of the tablets that were meant to fix me, chased it down with some straight Captain Morgan rum, and then waited.

When I started vomiting uncontrollably, I realized what I had done. I felt sick thinking that my mum would come down in the morning and find me there, and realized how fucked up that was. I wanted to call an ambulance so I could quietly go to hospital without anyone knowing, but then I thought the sirens would wake everyone up and stress everyone out.

I wanted everyone to stay calm because, in my mind, it wasn't a big deal. If I died, I died. If I lived, I lived. There was no point freaking out about it. I walked upstairs, calmly woke up my parents and said, "Don't freak out, but you need to take me to the hospital." They were obviously very confused and I explained I had taken too much of my lithium. Mum looked at me and said, "On purpose?" and when I replied yes, she got a look in her eyes that I'll never forget. Thinking about that expression is still enough for me to do everything in my power to try to prevent that night from ever happening again.

We went to the emergency department, and a nurse there rang the poisons department in Perth to get assistance. I passed out until morning. By 7 a.m. the next day, my best friend Sarah was messaging Mum trying to figure out what was going on. I didn't realize, but I had my Snapchat maps on; she had woken up and noticed I was at the hospital.

Within a couple of hours, all five of my best friends knew what was happening and were at the hospital to see me. One of my best friends, Sophie, was halfway to Esperance for a holiday with her boyfriend. When she got the phone call, she turned the car around to come back and see me, which is the perfect example of Sophie as a person: selfless and caring and always making me feel like I matter. I didn't want anyone to know because I didn't want anyone to think (mainly myself) that I was doing it for attention. My friends technically weren't allowed to see me because I was in the high dependency unit, but they convinced the nurses to let them in. Even though I didn't take those pills because I believed I was alone, knowing how many people truly cared made me feel a mixture of overwhelming love and guilt. My best friends and family are the best things to happen to me and they alone are worth being alive for.

I felt so awful that I put them through that, and I wish it hadn't taken me trying to hurt myself to realize I am more valuable alive. I have since realized suicide doesn't end your pain—it just passes it on to the people you love. I will never judge anyone who loses their battle to depression, but I left the hospital that day realizing that I still have a lot more fight left in me.

✧

Since that day, the bumper-car ride of mental illness hasn't got easier; I have just put in a lot of effort to learn how to cope with it. I have tried to see my therapist more and stay on top of my medication. Taking my meds has been, and will probably always be, my biggest struggle, and a lot of people living with bipolar have the same experience.

When times are good, I swear I don't have bipolar and don't need my lithium; when times finally become bad again, as they inevitably do with a mood disorder, I swear I'll start taking them again. The cycle repeats and repeats. I don't know why it is so hard for me to accept I have bipolar. I truly believe sometimes that I have constructed this mental illness as an excuse for shitty behavior, and once again stop taking my medication as a result—even though I have been diagnosed by multiple people and have most of the symptoms. This part of my mental health journey is still in the works, but my only regret is not taking it seriously sooner. If I had got a handle on it earlier, I might not have hurt people on the way.

Since that day there have been many times I have sat back and thought, *I am so glad I am here for this*—not here as in attending an event, but here as in alive. I am so glad my attempt didn't work because if it had, I wouldn't be here to experience so many moments.

If my demons had won that day, I would never have met Jake, my current boyfriend, who brings me so much joy—I have finally learned what a healthy relationship and true love feels like with him. I would have missed so many amazing memories with my loved ones, I would have never got a book deal, I would never have signed another TV series and be paid to do what I love, and I would have never learned that life is a gift. I know exactly how it feels to believe the only way to get past the darkness is to leave the earth, but I promise you there will always be one more moment that makes you say, 'I am so glad I stayed.' I now live for those moments.

One thing that my relationship with Jake has taught me is that it's not your partner's job to save you. They are there to hold your hand through the darkness, and their love can shine a light when the room is dark—but it is your job to walk out of that room. In the past I used partners as bandaids, but relying on your partner for happiness is toxic. They cannot be your only avenue of joy.

All the partners I'd had before Jake were used to fill a void. Once I filled that void myself with therapy, taking my proper medication, prioritizing a healthy lifestyle, and finally getting my mental health sorted, Jake came floating into my life. If I had met him when I didn't love myself and was depressed, our relationship would have reflected that. I love myself and that means I can accept the love of someone else.

When Jake and I met, true to form it went hard and fast. I met him on a Friday and by the Sunday I had his initials tattooed in a love heart on my foot. It was a home job tattoo by one of Jake's friends and when we were getting it done, our friend Kaili was looking at us, shaking her head and saying, "This will either be the dumbest thing you've both ever done or a bloody great story." As she was saying it, I knew it would be a damn good story, one I would never regret. The next day, I rang Mum and Dad to tell them about the tattoo and Dad said, "Of course you did." It was pretty on brand for me.

I love coincidences that are like little notes from the universe trying to grab your attention. The day before Jake and I met, I sat in the pub with my best friend Sarah and, out of the blue, said, "I want to marry a farmer." She replied, "Okay, random, but okay."

Little did I know that Jake, a dairy farmer (ironic because I am a vegan) was 600 kilometers from his home in Kambalda (a small town out of Kalgoorlie) in Grass Valley, buying a motorbike from my family on the farm I'd lived on for all those years—a bike I had ridden before. He had answered a Gumtree ad my cousin put up about a dirt bike, and out of every dirt bike for sale in the state, Jake decided to travel six hours to buy that one. When Jake was at the farm, my uncle saw him do a huge wheelie up their driveway. I guess Jake wasn't expecting he'd be getting this man's niece's initials tattooed three days later.

That day, my cousin asked Jake if he knew Tyler Mahoney because I was also from Kalgoorlie; Jake said, "Nope, never met her," bought the bike, and drove back to Kambalda, just missing my parents, who were staying at the farm that night. The next day we met in Kalgoorlie.

It's so refreshing to be in a relationship where there are no games. Jake was upfront with his emotions straight away and so was I. One thing I love about him is that he makes everything so easy; relationships have hard moments, and they take work, but I have never had to change who I am or my values to suit the relationship.

I began my journey with self-love and loving my body. It is such a struggle but really is worth it. Once I started to heal, I gained weight but also realized that it truly didn't matter. I was happy and making memories, and that was so much more important than fitting my size 6 jeans.

Back in my modeling days, I once heard the analogy that eating a bad meal was like dropping your phone—it's not ideal but you can pick it up and dust it off—but eating dessert after that meal is like dropping your phone and then stepping on it; why on earth would you do that? So, of course, I gave up dessert. Still to this day, eating ice-cream after dinner is a fifteen-minute argument in my own mind. It's back and forth between the pros and cons, telling myself I lack discipline, reassuring myself that one ice-cream won't make me fat, getting angry at myself because why do I think being fat is the worst thing ever? Reminding myself I am so much more than my body, deciding I could just have a banana, listing all the food I ate that day and questioning if I have eaten too many calories to have dessert, and then getting excited when I remember I skipped lunch. All the while, the freezer door is beeping because I have been down the rabbit hole of disordered eating for so long. I took clean eating to the extreme; my cheat meals used to be homemade curry with store-bought sauce. Store-bought sauce was a cheat for me because for so long, the diet industry slammed clean eating down my throat and disguised cutting out food groups as "healthy."

The number of memories and the amount of joy I missed out on because I thought the coolest thing about me was my abs breaks my heart. It has taken me four years to get to a point now where I have finally realized my body is to be enjoyed. The thoughts are always there, but I now actively choose happiness over a flat stomach.

I exercise and eat healthy now not for how they make me look, but for how they make me feel. It is so hard under extreme beauty standards and the patriarchy to truly believe your value is not measured by your weight, but I have realized it's a worthy battle. I know I am beautiful and that it is still the least interesting thing about me. I am so proud that I am now in a place where I can have the bad thoughts about my body come in and not listen to them anymore.

Living back in Kalgoorlie and full-time prospecting with my family, I am now working our leases in Kanowna only a couple of kilometers from where the Mahoneys first set up Mahoney's Diner over one hundred years ago. The universe had done a full circle, and I like to take those moments as signs that I am exactly where I am supposed to be. I became the loader operator, one of my favorite jobs I have ever had, as well as the person on the metal detector.

True prospectors know how to read the ground, find the gold, and how best to process it. We move between scrape and detecting, heap leaches, dry blowing, wet plants, rock crushing, and other processes, depending on what the gold is doing. I learn something every single day at work, and no day looks the same. It's great because I always have something new to teach my Prospectors Club members.

Human connection is one of the wonders we get to experience while here on earth. It's something I have searched for my whole life, wherever I go, and it's a big part of why I love country towns, where community is the lifeblood of a place. I am often moved by acts of humanity and drawn to people who are also seeking human connection. Traveling small town to small town in Australia has made me realize just how important a sense of community can be to some people, myself included. Most of my best memories have been created in small country towns and with the people in them.

I love being vulnerable with strangers and friends; I have learned that vulnerability is one of the fastest ways to form an honest, genuine human connection. The people who offer me vulnerability are always the ones I connect with the deepest and the fastest. We are all on this journey together and I think people feel safe when they know others have struggles as well. Vulnerability can lead to empathy and compassion: two things that I believe are paramount in a human connection. If you can feel another human's emotions or at least acknowledge the pain they are feeling, it opens the door to a selfless relationship.

I don't know why I feel the need to connect with everyone on a deeper level and I don't know why I look for human connection in every possible corner, but I think a big reason is that I have been at extreme lows where I couldn't imagine living another day; to think about another person experiencing those feelings breaks my heart.

Everyone has a story and it's amazing the similarities we share when you really listen to someone. I am extremely lucky that I have enough physical and mental resources to share with people who need it. I know not everyone feels as deep a need for this as me, but every time I have shared energy, whether it be physical or mental, I have received it tenfold in return. I have always found myself getting attached to people's lives and their journeys. I don't think its necessarily a bad thing, but I do always find myself analyzing people and how they got to where they are, and all the ins and outs of their identity. It's given me the ability to have deep conversations with people I meet.

The gold world is a tough place to try and make it. Prospecting is hard; it's unpredictable, inconsistent, tough work, and gold fever turns people wild—but I am so proud to be a part of it. Challenging the stereotypes around who is respected in this game is something I take great pride in. I count my lucky stars every day that I get to work with my family finding gold in our outback, worlds away from Fashion Week in Sydney or a catwalk in Melbourne or running events in Perth. It took me a lot of different roads to get back home, but I did.

Some of my favorite moments in life are when the universe does a full circle. I don't believe in coincidences; I believe they are purposeful signs from the universe pushing you in the right direction—a note from above telling you that you are exactly where you are supposed to be. I've always followed these signs and made note of when they appear.

I have had a few full-circle moments in my life that made me smile. In winter 2021, my brother, father, and I were on a ten-day prospecting trip 500 kilometers from home, on a station we spent a lot of time at as kids. On the way in we had spent about an hour on dirt tracks, and we drove past an old, abandoned shack and it sparked a deep memory in me I had forgotten about. I turned to Reece and told him that shack was where we used to sleep, and that creek was the one we used to play in. There were a heap of dongas missing, but that was 100 percent it. We were only nine and seven the last time we visited, but after seventeen years all the nostalgia started flowing.

Dad, Reece, and I spent the next ten minutes reliving all the memories from the station we once considered a home away from home. I remembered it being so much bigger and grander, but nonetheless it still brought all the memories racing in. I remembered staying there with our station friends Ben and Chelsea, and their dad, the caretaker.

It was on this station in the middle of the Australian outback, about five hours from Kalgoorlie, that we spent hours chasing bulls, riding bikes, making cubby houses, and following Mum and Dad around the bush. Seventeen years later I was back here as a full-time prospector with Reece and Dad.

We set up camp not far from the shack. The area is harsh: big ranges; dry creek beds; no gumtrees, only shrub, grass, and salt bush; and the odd water trough for the cattle. It's so different from the Kalgoorlie goldfields. The geology is very different, featuring big ironstone ridges, but I still feel so at home.

Dad had been there a couple weeks prior and had found a speccy (a specimen, gold mixed with rock) on the top of the hill. He wasn't going to detect the hill but needed phone service to make a call, so walked to the top, made the work call and called me to say hello. Dad says I'm clutching at straws, but I think even that is a coincidence in itself. As he walked back down the hill, he decided to turn on his detector and ended up finding a 1-ounce ironstone specimen on the way down.

Reece and I began chaining the hill while Dad kept searching for more virgin patches. Reece found another 4 ounces in ironstone speccies, and I found a little nugget. As the sun was going down, I hit a faint target directly up the hill and in line with the speccies, 30 centimeters from Reece's chain lines (I won't let him live that one down). At first, I thought it was ground noise, but my excitement levels began to rise as we hit calcite and the signal became quite loud. The signal getting louder as we got deeper meant it wasn't ground noise, and the fact that the signal was under the calcite meant it wasn't rubbish. It was gold, we just weren't sure how much. We try to avoid the two-way radios when out bush unless it's vital, to ensure other people who may be in the area can't hear us—but Reece and I both agreed this was worth calling the old man over for.

He would kill me for saying this, but he struggled up the hill, huffing and puffing, the smokes and old age finally showing. As he reached us he said, "This better be fucking worth it." Reece and I laughed and I said, "Well, we think we've found the source of the speccies." It was almost a joke, but with some underlying hope we might be right.

Finding the source is on the rarer side, but this target was exactly where it should be—it was almost too easy and too good to be true. Dad laughed and said, "Yeah, right. Wouldn't that be nice?" As we began to chip away at the calcite, we all took turns with the pick, and all took turns repeating the infamous prospector saying: "Fucking calcite." It's as hard as concrete and an absolute pain in the arse.

We got deeper and the target got louder. This is one of my favorite moments as a prospector: you know you have hit gold and you know it's a good target. We were all laughing, digging out the hole and trying to guess the size of what we had found, and I thought to myself, *God, I love my job.* It's those moments that make all the hard ones worth it. You forget the goldless days, the flies, the heat; that hit of dopamine comes rushing in. It's the moment that is addictive. This high truly makes me forget all the lows.

We were digging in the calcite when we hit gold—not what we were expecting but exactly what we were hoping for. It wasn't a decent-sized nugget—it was very rough, attached to ironstone and only around a gram—but when we pulled it out, there was still a great signal in the hole. We had hit an ironstone reef. For once the gold was exactly where it was supposed to be, and it all made sense. Gold likes to play tricks sometimes, but that day it didn't.

We were all over the moon and we stayed up until midnight hacking away, following the reef as it moved through the ground, making sure we didn't lose it. The ironstone we were pulling out was littered with visible gold, and the richest parts of the reef were so packed with gold that Dad had said it was the richest he had ever seen by a long mile. It was running at kilos per tonne. If the old boys had found something that rich, they would have said they had found the mother lode.

We spent the next forty-eight hours hand-digging out as much paydirt and reef as we were allowed before heading home to process it. On the last night, we were sitting around the hole having a Baileys and coffee break, which is a must. We all laughed about some of the crazy stuff we would get up to out there as kids, and how wild it was that seventeen years later us three were sitting around an ironstone reef, working as a family of full-time prospectors, keeping the tradition alive. One of the reasons I came back to prospecting after leaving was to preserve my family's history; I think Na would be so proud to see her granddaughter pursuing her passion as a full-time job. We ended up getting 15 ounces from that reef, no small amount—but to be back in my childhood playground finding gold with my family for a living was a priceless full-circle moment that I will remember forever.

I turned to Dad and said, "When you and Mum would take us here as kids, did you think that seventeen years later, we would be back and working as full-time prospectors together?"

He paused for a moment, took a sip of his Baileys, laughed and said, "Nope, I didn't think you were both that fucking stupid."

You must be some sort of stupid to be a full-time gold prospector, but I wouldn't change it for the world.

15

DREDGING UP THE PAST

Can you be friends with an ex? Or more to the point—can you have a healthy working relationship with your boss after having a failed intimate relationship with them? After I was asked to come back and work on *Parker's Trail* New Zealand, I realized this was something I'd have to figure out quickly if I wanted to continue my *Gold Rush* career. Anxiety, awkwardness, and anticipation were all racing through my mind when I got on a flight to see Parker twelve months after our relationship had ended. There was a lot on the line and a lot that could go wrong; we would be living and working with each other for three months, spending every waking moment together while filming a TV show. It was already an intense, bizarre situation, and would be magnified by the fact that not only had we been in an intimate relationship when we last saw each other, but we also hadn't spoken at all for about eight months. Sure, we had both moved on and were happily in new relationships—but we had never been around each other in a purely platonic setting. We had to figure out our new dynamic quick smart if we were going to make a TV show together.

The new year of 2021 was an opportunity for *Parker's Trail* to continue. Of course, the pandemic was still a threat, so I thought the chances were thin. It would be a logistical nightmare, and the fact Parker and I had barely spoken in eight months certainly didn't give me hope. I had various phone calls with producers, and they were pushing hard to make it happen but I had my doubts. Even if they asked me back, Western Australia's borders were still closed; I wasn't sure how they would even get me out of Kalgoorlie.

Craig and I had a phone call, and he told me that the *Trail* would be a mission to pull off with the state of international travel and border restrictions, let alone while making sure none of the crew got COVID. He then asked the question I had been dreading, one that gave me an instant lump in my throat: he asked if I had spoken to Parker. I paused, and we both knew the awkwardness of the situation.

"No," I replied. "Not for a while."

Craig sighed and told me I should reach out to him. He reassured me that production wanted me to be on Season 5 of the *Trail*, himself included, but it was up to Parker at the end of the day.

Even though I thought I knew Parker very well, I was still nervous. He wouldn't let our failed romantic journey impact my time on the show, would he? There was only one way to find out, so I swallowed my pride and sent him a text. His response was short and superficial—texting was never his strong suit—and our conversation didn't exactly reassure me that I would be back on the *Trail*. I just had to wait and see if I got the call. Being on TV has its perks, but its uncertainty is not one of them.

I tried to get on with normal life while I waited. Finally, one morning I was at work, pushing scrapes in the loader (on the hunt for gold as usual) when I checked my phone and saw I had a missed call from the *Trail* production team. My stomach tightened from the anxiety of the unknown. I left work and drove back into town to get better reception so I could return the call. Craig answered the phone and, surprisingly, said the *Trail* had been greenlit, which was huge considering just how hard the logistics would be. He didn't give me much more information except that I had a scheduled video call with Danny and Parker in two days to find out where we were going and what my role would be (depending on whether Parker was actually going to ask me back). The video call made me nervous; I had no idea how our new platonic relationship would look.

Over those two days, my anxiety set up camp and was a bitch to kick out, so on the day of the call, I was relieved to see Danny was there. He had always been a safe space for me, so having him to buffer the conversation and relieve any awkward moments made me feel at ease. I also felt angry that I had let my relationship with Parker get to a space that made me feel uncomfortable. Our friendship had been so great, but, in that moment, I felt like I was answering the call from a stranger. I just hoped things would be "normal."

As soon as I answered the phone, Parker dived straight into it by asking me to come to New Zealand with him and Danny. He wanted me to organize the mine sites we would visit, and get contacts in the

New Zealand mining game. I was hesitant—it was a huge job and, in true *Gold Rush* style, I had three weeks to get it done—but the phone call was exciting, and it was a huge relief that I would be going on my second *Parker's Trail* season.

Even though it was a positive phone call, the energy between Parker and me was awkward. I think we didn't quite know how to act with each other. Craig later told me that while Parker had owned up to dropping the ball on communicating it to me, he had also said, "Of course I want Tyler back on the *Trail*." Knowing this eased my thoughts about us continuing a working relationship, which was lucky—with only three weeks to organize our itinerary and make our New Zealand connections, there was no time to waste on worrying. I started preparing that very night.

Missing bags, canceled flights, multiple COVID tests, five layovers, and one bus ride later, I finally hit New Zealand hotel quarantine. It was an absolute feat by production to get us there. In New Zealand, not only were there ten compulsory days of quarantine in a hotel room, the location of which was designated to you once you landed there, but to get one of these quarantine rooms, you basically entered a lottery. Kiwi residents weren't given priority, and even if you had applied several times, you didn't get any extra consideration. Whether we would get to New Zealand or not all depended on luck. . . and we had thirty people who all needed quarantine rooms, or the show wasn't going ahead. They were nightmarish odds, but luckily, the *Gold Rush* gods were looking out for us. Even though some of us weren't approved until two days before flying out, we all managed to get a room.

I was sent to Hamilton on the North Island to complete my quarantine, and on day one, Danny set up a group chat between me, him, Parker, and Jeff (who had replaced Fred). We video-called as a group every day to get to know Jeff better and to catch up. It had been over two years since Danny and I had seen each other, and we picked up right where we left off. Parker and I kept things superficial, though. I was still unsure how it would be between Parker and me in person, but I had put myself in this position, so I had to put my big-girl pants on and suck it up.

I managed to survive being locked in a room by myself for ten days with zero mental breakdowns, and the day finally came to see Parker in real life for the first time in two years. What I was hoping would happen did: Parker and I slipped instantly into a great friendship with no awkward moments. While it helped that we still had a lot in common, I credit our new friendship to both of us putting our ego and emotions aside, and just getting on with it.

This made things a lot easier, and we spent the next three months exploring NZ and having the adventure of a lifetime. There was a lot of hard work involved, of course. We worked very long days, and were also on a mission to find the specific wash plant Parker was looking for. This all being filmed added another layer of complexity. Even though it was at times exhausting, we couldn't believe how lucky we all were to be exploring such a beautiful country. Swimming with great white sharks, bungee jumping, skydiving, canyoning, and jetboating are just a few of the amazing things we got to experience while on the *Trail*. We also got to meet some great miners, and saw a lot of great gold too. As clichéd as it is, my favorite takeaway from the *Trail* is the friendships I made. Danny, Parker, and I became such a tight unit, and I think that special bond translates through the TV screen.

Frederique and Sheena were two of the producers on the *Trail,* and also became two of my closest friends. After a lifetime of being surrounded by men, it was really refreshing to have two strong women to work with. The TV world is similar to the mining world in that it's a male-dominated industry, so we had a lot of shared experiences and quickly became close as we experienced some amazing things together.

Those three months flew by, and it wasn't long before we came to one of our last locations, which was also one of my favorites: Pauanui in the North Island. We had left the *Lord of the Rings*–esque forests and mountains of the South Island, and had landed in the warm, tropical surf coast of the North. On our day off, we all headed into town, and rode bikes to the beach, where we spent the afternoon on rented surfboards. It was just what we needed after spending most of our time in bush mine sites.

Our accommodation for that night seemed like paradise: a tucked-away mountainside resort with ocean views. We all had our own little cabins in the rainforest, as well as a pool, a tennis court, and a restaurant with a balcony that looked over the ocean. I was extremely homesick and missing my boyfriend like crazy at this point, but tried to enjoy the last of the trip. We had just finished a long day of filming when Parker asked Danny, Sheena, Frédérique— aka Fred—and me to dinner. This wasn't uncommon—us five always hung out together—but the formal invitation was interesting.

After freshening up for dinner, Fred, Sheena, and I walked up the restaurant stairs to see Danny and Parker both dressed in button-up shirts, about to pop a nice bottle of champagne. As soon as I saw Parker dressed up, I knew something was going on. It was a rare occasion to see him looking so fancy. Us three girls sat down with the two boys with a look of confusion on our faces.

I looked directly at Parker and said, "Okay, this is weird. What's going on?"

He and Danny laughed, and Parker said, "I have a proposition for you."

I was still very confused. Why were Fred and Sheena here? Why couldn't Parker just ask me tomorrow at breakfast? What was with the expensive champagne? I was equally nervous and excited.

Parker began by saying that he had invited Danny, Sheena, and Fred to be here as well because he wanted me to have a support network to bounce ideas off, to give me advice, and to help me make decisions—because he knew that sometimes I lack the ability to think things through, and say yes without thinking about any consequences. So he invited our friends, who could talk me through my response to his proposition, and prevent me from making any rash decisions.

We popped the champagne, and with a smirk Parker said, "Tyler, I want you to come and help run my new Alaskan operation."

A wave of excitement hit me. Without missing a beat, I said, "Absolutely!"

Everyone laughed and Parker firmly said, "No, this is exactly what I didn't want. It's going to be a big commitment, and you would have to make some sacrifices. I really want you to think this through." I looked to Danny, Sheena, and Fred for help because I didn't need any time to think about this—it was an easy yes for me—but they quickly jumped in and started asking Parker the important questions about money, timing, and responsibilities. I am grateful that Parker asked them to be there, and I am grateful that they asked the questions I need to care about. I was always taught to walk through every door that opened for you and figure out the rest on the fly, but that isn't always the most logical thing to do.

Over the next hour or so, we drank nice wine and ate good food while we discussed what the next mining season would be like for us, as well as all the excitement that comes with new ventures. In the past, Parker and I had briefly discussed turning the gold he mined into jewelry and selling it. The market to sell it was there, but he just didn't have enough time to do it; with my ecommerce and jewelry background, it made sense to join forces. We all got excited over the prospect of this, and I explained that it would be my dream job. I missed making jewelry so much, and this would allow me to enjoy that creative process but still be involved in the worlds of TV and gold. It was such a great dinner. We were all so happy, and I felt so excited to be taking the next step in my career.

Danny reiterated that what I was saying yes to would be full-on. I would essentially have three jobs: helping run the Alaskan operation (which would turn out to be one of the hardest jobs I'd ever have), starting the new jewelry company with Parker and filming the next season of the TV show. It was going to be a big year, but I knew it was exactly what I was supposed to do.

Then it hit me: there would be no way I could continue The Prospector's Club membership and do all of this. The high of the night started to slip for me when I came to the realization that after working so hard to build the Club up for the last three years, I would have to let it go. I vocalized this to the group, and they all agreed that there was no way I could run the Club on top of this new role. I wasn't ready to let go of the Club at all; it was like my child, and we were still growing so quickly. The community I had created was so special, but I knew Parker's opportunity was too big to let go of. I knew I had to pivot the Club to make it work, but I would.

Parker asked one last time, "Are you sure you want to do this? You'll be away from your family and friends, and there will be some really hard times and big sacrifices."

I was certain in my decision: "I'm in."

I was so excited when I woke up the next morning. Running a small business is so hard and financially unstable, and being a gold prospector or working on TV is the exact same—I never knew if the money would dry up overnight. Despite this, I'd always had this deep knowing that my career path would naturally progress if I just kept working at it, and I finally felt like it was. I also felt like Parker and I would eventually take the next step in our working relationship as long as we didn't let our personal history get in the way, which we had clearly done well. It had been hard, but I felt like we had reached a place of great respect for each other. We had finally cracked the code to being not only colleagues but friends with an ex. I was very proud of us both.

The first thing I did after that dinner was ring Jake. As I dialed his number, I had the thought that this might be a bit of a blow for him—it would mean doing long distance, something that I knew from experience could seriously impact our relationship. I would never let a man hold me back in my career, but Jake meant the world to me. It was important that he was comfortable with the situation. I was so worried that he would react with jealousy or insecurity, or rightfully be unsure of how a long-distance relationship between us would work.

A wave of anxiety hit me as he answered the phone, but as I told him the news, all those worries disappeared. He responded in such a confident, mature, and supportive way, and I will forever be so grateful that he never made me choose between him and my career. He was ecstatic for me, which was a huge relief. I told him it would mean we would spend most of 2022 apart from each other, and he said, "What's one year away from each other when we will have another sixty after it?" That is Jake to a tee. I then rang my parents and brother, who were, of course, beyond proud and excited. They have always been my biggest fans, and are the biggest reason I feel so confident in pursuing my dreams. I know they will always be there if things don't work out, and that is such a privilege.

I immediately began trying to figure out a game plan on how to pivot The Prospector's Club. I knew in my heart that it wasn't time to close the business, but I also knew there was no way I could continue the current model. I had to come up with a plan that would keep the business rolling, but cut down the workload. I also wasn't ready to give up the money. Even though the plan with Parker would be a great financial move for me, I couldn't 100 percent rely on it following through. TV work is tumultuous, and though it being canceled was unlikely, it'd be unwise to cut off my income before I was receiving it from the next source.

I had been reading a lot about passive income, and knew this was where I needed to direct the Club to. I had already made some passive income from the blog (through AdSense money) and from selling my ebooks, but I had three years' worth of knowledge, interviews, videos, and lessons included in the Club's membership. I needed to rebrand it, and turn it into passive income. Luckily, I knew exactly what to do, and stayed up all night writing a business plan.

"The Treasure Chest" was the next move for the Club. The Chest was going to be a purchasable file that would be automatically sent to the customer after payment. It would contain every single video, interview, lesson, and piece of information ever made and shared over the last three years in the Club membership; there was so much priceless information in that membership—over 160 videos—and now it wouldn't go to waste. It only took me two weeks to make. After all, I had spent three years unknowingly creating the content! Plus, once all the hard work was done, there would be almost zero future effort: no shipping, no packaging, no writing, no lesson planning. All I had to worry about was managing my socials, keeping up the marketing, and caring for my customers. It was the perfect way to utilize all the hard work I had already done.

With everything I had going on, the *Trail* was over before we knew it. The ten weeks had flown by, and it was time for all of us to head back home. Before we all went our separate ways across the globe, production threw us a wrap party that was one of the best I have been to. A wrap party is a party that production throws the cast and crew once filming has finished. For this party, they hired us a boat and we had a huge party on the ocean in a little bay just outside of Auckland. Filming a whole TV series is extremely hard work—so you can imagine that everyone was ready to let their hair down. We partied all afternoon and then headed into the production studio, where our local production company had their own private bar. We partied into the early hours of the morning. The next morning, after the hangover of a lifetime, we were then taken to explore wineries and beaches on an island off the coast of New Zealand, a treat that production had organized for finishing the series early. It was a dream. After, we all parted for our flights, but this time, it wasn't a "goodbye"—it was a "see you soon."

I touched down on home soil completely exhausted. Even though the trip was filled with fun times, working and living with the same people for three months straight is exhausting enough without constantly being in front of a camera with a microphone around your neck. I didn't have time to rest, though; I only had six weeks at home before I was back on a plane, so I went straight into planning mode. The problem was that getting a US working visa was an effort, and I was lucky to have a team of Discovery Channel lawyers doing the hard yards for me. The final step in the visa process was when we hit our biggest hurdle: for my visa to be approved, I needed an in-person meeting at a US embassy. Of course, we were still in the thick of pandemic restrictions; Perth and Sydney had both shut their embassies for an undisclosed amount of time, and the next available appointment in Melbourne was six months away, which would mean I would miss the US mining season.

We tried absolutely everything, from pulling strings to get a meeting to letters from lawyers to let me send my passport away instead of meeting in person. All efforts failed, and I felt the chance of me taking the job in Alaska with Parker slipping away—until I had the great idea to try a US embassy in a different country, which a lot of Aussies were doing at the time. The next available appointment in the closest country was Fiji, so I emailed the Discovery lawyer who agreed it was the best plan of attack. Within a week, I was on a flight to Fiji.

I flew from Kalgoorlie via Perth, Brisbane, and Nadi to Suva, where I got a taxi to a hotel in the city center. It wasn't quite like the Fijian resorts you see on Instagram, but I didn't care—I just wanted that appointment. The next day, I called a cab and gave the driver a big cash tip to take me to an ATM to withdraw my money, and then to a post office to pay for the appointment. All went well, and the appointment was booked for five days' time. Everything was looking great until I woke up on the day of the meeting to an email from the embassy: my appointment had been canceled. I was devastated. I didn't want to go home. I had everything riding on this new job in Alaska. Cue the next great idea: I knew I still had a working visa for Canada, so I rang Parker and production. I said I would fly to Parker's Canadian mine, and we would sort out the US visa while I was there. Parker was short-staffed and needed help in the Yukon anyway, so it worked out well.

The US embassies in Canada didn't have any available appointments for another four months, which was way too late, but I hopped on a flight trusting that I would somehow make it work. I flew from Suva to Nadi, LA, Vancouver, Whitehorse, and, finally, Dawson, a remote northern town. I caught up with Fred, who was working at Parker's mine site as a field producer. I was exhausted but so excited to be reunited with her and get started on my new journey. Summer was on its way, the snow had nearly melted away, the sun wasn't setting until 3 a.m. and Dawson was starting to fill with TV crew, miners, and tourists. Dawson in the summer is one of the best places to be; it's a weird mixture of blue-collar miners, hippies escaping society, and British people there to film a TV show. Somehow, they all live and work together with ease—alcohol being a good middleman.

Meanwhile, Parker was being slightly sheepish with me and not giving me a lot of information about essential stuff, like whether I even had a room at camp. After a conversation with Fred, I quickly realized why: while it's all well and good to offer his ex-girlfriend a job, he was nervous to have his ex-girlfriend and his current girlfriend living and working together. It was understandable, but his way of dealing with the situation was to simply not address it. Had he told his girlfriend I was coming? Had he even told her about me and our past? Would she be there? I was firing these questions at Fred as we walked to get coffee in Dawson. She had no idea, but she did tell me that Parker had said the whole thing was "a nightmare." Fred and I laughed at that. I thought back to when Parker and I were dating—I would have never imagined this would be a position I'd find myself in.

As we arrived at the coffee shop, reality hit me right in the face. Parker's girlfriend was standing right out the front, because of course she was. Having Instagram-stalked her, I obviously knew exactly who she was.

"Oh, God," Fred whispered.

"Fuck me," I responded.

I was so nervous to meet Parker's new girlfriend, and outside a coffee shop was not how I imagined it going down. Before I even had time to think about how I was going to approach the situation, we were standing awkwardly in front of each other. As soon as we said hello, I knew she knew exactly who I was, and she knew I knew who she was. We exchanged introductions and awkwardly parted ways. Even though I had completely moved on from Parker and was in a very happy relationship, my ego was a little hurt. It was hard for me to meet the girl who took my place, even if it was a place I no longer wanted. Of course, I got myself into this awkward position, so I swallowed my pride and got on with things.

The next two months were a whirlwind. I was living in a mining camp in northern Canada, 14,000 kilometers from home, filming a TV show with my ex-boyfriend. I loved camp life; Parker's Yukon crew were amazing, and I feel like I fit in instantly. His crew were young and fun, and so were the TV crew who also lived on the claim five minutes up the hill from us. Thankfully, Parker's girlfriend and I were getting along super well, and my friendship/working relationship with Parker was only strengthening. My time was split between the office, where Parker was giving me various responsibilities, and in the cut, where I was running equipment. In true Parker style, he had me hauling dirt in a rock truck with barely any training. To be fair, he was understaffed and needed help, which was what I came over to do—so even if sitting in a rock truck for twelve hours a day wasn't really my jam, I didn't mind.

Before I knew it, I managed to get a visa appointment in Vancouver, and was on a flight out of Dawson down to the big smoke. I was so sad to leave all my new friends at the mine site, but I was ready to start the next chapter in Alaska. Parker told me we would be in Alaska for six weeks mining the ground, and would then return to Canada to finish off the season there. On that note, I packed my bags and said my goodbyes without knowing just what I was walking into, and just how crazy the next ten weeks were going to be.

It didn't matter what lay in Alaska, though, because Parker and the rest of the team had my back. I knew at this point that Parker trusted me—*really* trusted me—and that meant so much after everything we'd both put in to building our professional relationship, as well as working on our friendship. Most importantly, after all the hard work I had put into my career and myself, I was ready to face all the challenges ahead of me. Bring it on, Alaska—I knew I could handle it.

EPILOGUE

Living just below the Arctic Circle, my life looked like it never had
before: extreme seasons, wild Alaskans, grizzly bears, wolves, and
guns. Among it all, I was doing a job I had absolutely no experience
with while being broadcast on international television. If I fucked up,
the shame didn't stay in the company—it was a free-for-all across just
about every continent. I was doing so many things I had no history in:
excavator operating, MSHA compliance, pump maintenance, water
management, navigating lease agreements that were different from
back home, to name a few. We were a small team, meaning everyone
had to be a jack of all trades—including me. Parker put me in charge
of hiring the team, which made me extremely nervous. I have never
hired people for a placer mine before, and to make it worse, I had to
hire them remotely. We were inundated with thousands of resumés,
and I had no idea where to begin. I rang Parker and asked what I
should be looking for in these new hires; he gave a quick sigh and
said, "Just make sure they have a good attitude." *Great*, I thought to

myself. It took me two days of phone calls and trusting my gut, but I managed to hire three miners, gave them five days to get to Alaska and start work, and then hoped for the best.

Before the end of the following week I had organized accommodation, insurance, lease compliance, MSHA compliance, and appropriate training for everyone. I had also started setting up all of our first aid, mine signage, and mine safety equipment, and created all of the needed gold-tracking spreadsheets, completed all of our miner onboarding, set up payroll, and got all of our paperwork in order to be a legal mine. Finally, we could begin digging.

Just when I thought I had my anxiety under control, it came racing back in as it always loves to do—except this time, I had processes in place to keep it at bay. Besides, even though I was anxious about the season ahead, I felt a wave of excitement when I watched the first holes being dug. The enormous behind-the-scenes work to get to that point had all been worth it. As Parker and I stood looking over the cut, I asked him if he thought we would do well and find a worthy amount of gold. He turned to me and said, "I hope so, but it depends how good the miners you hired are," and he walked off. I love working with Parker, but he tends to throw people in the deep end. If you sink, you don't last long, but if you manage to swim, you can earn his trust. I had been keeping my head above water for the entirety of our relationship, and I hoped this wasn't the iceberg that would sink me.

Even though I have been gold mining my whole life, this was a completely different story. The gold was different, we were running a wash plant—which was a different beast to our dry blowers—and then there was the water management. Being from the desert, I had never seen how much of a pain in the arse getting water out of a mine could be. On top of the new miners, Parker hired a foreman, Mark, who was the best thing for that operation. Mark had years of experience moving dirt, operating machinery, and managing people, and had a lot of local contacts. If it wasn't for him, I honestly don't think we would have been able to mine.

The ground was also very different to what Parker was used to in the Yukon, and it brought a whole lot of challenges. We had a very late start due to myriad reasons, so we were fighting against the clock every single day. Winter was coming, and we had to fight to get the paydirt out and sluiced before we were frozen out. If we didn't, we were at risk of losing money, a situation I am very familiar with. Funnily enough, we had a smooth start. Things were going well on the mine site, surprisingly well for a new operation—it was just a shame that camp life was extremely tumultuous.

Being from outback Australia, I thought I knew the definition of the Wild West, but remote Alaska took it to a new level. I was already on edge being in the States during a time of political unrest, when citizens were having their reproductive rights stripped away. It was hard enough for me to relax, and, in true gold-world style, within a week we had our first robbery: a car was stolen from our camp. The gold may be different in Australia, but the greed and the people involved aren't. Don't get me wrong, there are some amazing people in the gold game—but it really wasn't that long ago that killing people for being in your sluice box was still legal in Alaska, as a lot of the locals liked to remind me. They also liked to remind me that we were mining on private property so if we saw someone who shouldn't be there, we should "just shoot 'em."

The car was stolen from right under our noses, and it was an uneasy feeling for all of us knowing that we were in the middle of the woods and still at risk; I was in a management position and felt very responsible for keeping the crew, the equipment, and the gold safe. Had locals found out where we were staying? I decided to stay as quiet as possible online about my whereabouts, and I told the boys to keep quiet about who and where we were when they were talking to locals at the bars.

Within the week it happened again, this time in broad daylight— except it wasn't a stolen car but a smashed window and a stolen TV from the cabin next to our dorms. This was enough for production and Parker to react. Production's response was to hire an armed guard to patrol the property every night, and to install security cameras. Parker's response was much more extreme in my eyes, but he and everyone else thought it was very necessary: he showed up to the site and handed me a Glock. Within two weeks of being in America, I was forced to carry a gun on me. The miners explained that they all had guns as well—one of the miners pulled a loaded handgun out of his jacket pocket then and there! Keep in mind that Parker and the crew are American, while I am Australian; this was the biggest culture shock I experienced moving to the States, but between the crime we were experiencing and our remote location, I understood why. At night I would put my Glock on my bedside table. Sleeping next to a loaded gun was a first for me, and not something I ever thought I would have to do.

✦

If it wasn't criminals I was worrying about, it was the Alaskan wildlife. I had never in my life had to deal with large predators, and I was right bang in the middle of their home. When I asked locals if I ever had to worry about the number of wild animals in the valley, they always responded, "No, you'll probably be fine." There was *always* a "probably." For example, when I asked them if it was safe for me to go for afternoon walks, their response was always "you'll probably be fine, just take a dog and bear spray, and always tell someone where you're going and how long you'll be." They say Australia has the dangerous animals, but I never had to carry kangaroo spray with me in the outback.

I had seen my fair share of moose and black bears in Canada, but I had no experience with grizzlies and wolves—and, of course, we had both in the valley. There was a big grizzly reported to be hanging around our mine, which always kept me on my toes, and I was definitely not prepared for the fact we were staying next to a wolf den. Wolves are notorious for being elusive, so the number of wolf encounters I had made me feel very lucky; after I got over my initial fear, those moments turned into some of my fondest memories of Alaska. There are many Alaskans who go their whole lives without seeing wolves, and within one week I had multiple encounters. We were in a valley where the wolf packs hunted caribou, so they were very active at that time of year. My first encounter was when I was driving out to the mine and four large wolves crossed the road right in front of me. The pack leader, a big grey wolf, actually stopped and looked at me before continuing on its way. It made me realize just how huge wolves are, and I was thankful to be safely locked in my car. My luck continued the very next day: as I drove around the corner on a dirt road in the woods, I had to suddenly slam on my brakes; six wolf pups ran straight in front of my car and into the woods, maybe chasing their mum. Then, the next week, wolves howled throughout the night. It was magical.

Like I said before, water management was not my strong point. It would also end up being our biggest enemy. We spent the whole season fighting a losing battle against water determined to flood our cut, making it near impossible for us to get the paydirt out before winter hit. For weeks on end, we had three pumps dewatering the cut just to keep our heads above float. It was a nightmare. We had berms and dikes up trying to dam the water, but just as the pumps started to gain, a berm would bust and reflood the cut. By the end of the season, we were on a race against the clock to get the pay out before the cut flooded completely. If this happened, not only would we come out with barely any gold, but it would probably also be the end of my job with Parker.

Staying vigilant against the flooding meant that someone always had to be babysitting the pump, even during the night. I like to think I'm pretty tough, but when it comes to being alone at night, surrounded by wolves, in the woods where we had been robbed and had no phone reception, I was as weak as a kitten. Nonetheless, I had to suck it up and get on with it. I couldn't ask the miners to go straight from twelve-hour days to night shifts if I wasn't going to do it myself. So, we would all work from 7 a.m. to 7 p.m., break for dinner, and then start the night shifts. I took the longest shift (8 p.m.

to midnight) because I felt giving the worst shift to the miners would have been bad leadership. So, for four hours, I sat in the middle of the woods with no phone service, all by myself in the dark. I have never been so terrified in my life. I would see movements in the woods, or hear things coming from the trees. The miners reminded me I had a gun, and to just shoot any human or animal that came close to me— but somehow that didn't stop me being absolutely scared shitless.

I managed to survive the week of nightshifts without being mauled by a wolf or shot by a rogue gold robber, but the water was still coming in hard and fast; draining the cut felt like we were fighting a losing battle. We had to get the pay out of the ground before the walls burst and the water came flooding in, or the whole season would have been a waste. We were on borrowed time.

The cut had been split into two sections, with the bottom half richer in gold than the top half. It was a Friday night, and we had every machine in the cut frantically pulling pay before we lost the battle. We had water bursting through every ten minutes, so we would use the excavator to plug the holes just enough that the water would go from what looked like a burst water main to a dribbling tap. What started off as one or two leaks to monitor turned into ten to eleven. You could feel the anxiety in the air; everyone had their game faces on, and we were determined to win. When 7 p.m. came around, our normal knock-off time, we just looked at each other and knew we weren't going to stop. We only had about four hours of work left before all the pay from the bottom half was out. So we started working into the night. If we stopped, we would come back in the morning to a lake, not a mine site. Parker was making the nine-hour drive from the Yukon to help us, and when he got in around 9 p.m., he jumped straight into the excavator to help.

By the time midnight hit, we finally had all the bottom-half pay out. The equipment was switched off, and I felt like every single one of us took a sigh of relief. The lightness was back in the air again. The wolves began howling as we had a night cap before bed, ready to do it all over again the next day. Even though we managed to mine the richer half, there was still pay left in the cut, and we refused to finish the season with money left in the ground. Every miner knows there is no worse feeling.

Over the next day, we were still fighting an uphill battle with the water. It was so bad that we were mining 5 meters below our sump hole. I was stressed and homesick and just needed some alone time, so I took twenty minutes to go and sit in my car and video-call my boyfriend. When I looked out of my window, I noticed the producer was lurking around my car. I couldn't even have twenty minutes to myself without someone needing something! He asked me when I was going back over to the cut, and wanted to make sure I was wearing my microphone when I did. I wasn't thinking straight and just wanted to talk to my boyfriend, so I dismissively said I would be over soon. He kept lurking around my car, though, and that's when it hit me—if he was being this persistent about getting me over to the cut, there was a good chance something was going on. I wound down my window and asked if something had gone wrong. He said, "Things have changed in the cut." I knew he wouldn't tell me what was happening to ensure my reaction to whatever was happening would be authentic. I ended the call and made my way to the cut, praying it wasn't the water.

My fear was a reality, but it was worse than any of us could have pictured. There was a drift shaft, filled with water from melted permafrost, that we had no clue about—and we had just hit it with our excavator. It had exploded; I had never seen so much water moving so fast in my life. Parker was in meetings and wasn't answering his phone, and Mark had left to go find him, so it was just me and the boys trying to fight the rapid flood. We had one excavator trying to plug the hole and the other excavator trying to break the dam walls to release some pressure, while the dozer was moving dirt to try and redirect the water. The situation quickly became very dangerous; we had health and safety on standby with ropes, just in case any of the equipment slipped into the water and a miner needed to be saved.

It became evident very quickly that we were in a lot of trouble and a decision had to be made: pull the machinery and the pumps, and lose all the remaining pay—or put the miners and equipment at risk to save the gold. The decision had to be made very quickly. The miners were on the radio waiting for me to make the call, and I looked over at the safety guy, who was sternly shaking his head. I knew I had to pull it. "Evacuate now," I said firmly over the radio. We pulled the first excavator out in time, but the dozer and other excavator were stuck, and the water was rising quickly. Not only did we have to get them out, but we also had to get an excavator to the other end of the cut to pull all the pumps before the water hit them as well. With the help of the excavator, we dragged the dozer out. One of our miners, Jarred, who was only twenty-four, put his hand up to go down into the cut and attempt to walk the other excavator out. It was risky, but I also didn't want Parker to come back to one of his $400,000 excavators under water. We had health and safety right there as we all watched Jarred attempt to walk the machine out. His options were slim: walk it up the huge dam wall or go through the shallow end of the water. He chose the latter. We all held our breaths as the excavator dived into the water, nearly flooding the cab, before he swung the arm around and pulled himself and the machine to safety.

Parker and Mark got back just as it was time to pull the pumps, and we all knew right then and there that the season had just ended. There was no way we could pump the water out of the cut before winter would hit; we would be frozen out. It was a hard pill to swallow. Within an hour, the whole cut was 10 meters underwater. The next week was spent running the pay we managed to save through the wash plant, waiting anxiously to see if we found enough gold or if the season was a bust.

After months of endless work, it was the day of the final gold weigh and we were about to find out if our work had been fruitless or if we had found the mother lode. The miners, Parker, and I all stood around the scales with many cameras pointing in our direction; our mics were turned on and the producer gave us the green light to start pouring the gold onto the scales. As the gold from the final clean-up hit the scales, it wasn't hard to tell that it wasn't enough, and as the final gold speck hit the scale, we all sighed with disappointment. We had come in less than we'd hoped. In the gold game it was a feeling I had experienced my whole life, but it still didn't make it easy. Even though we didn't find as much gold as we had hoped, there were still a lot of wins to take out of Alaska and Parker was very happy and proud. We all did our best and unfortunately sometimes the gold just isn't there.

That was the end of that; my Alaskan adventure simultaneously felt like it had flashed by in a second and like I had spent a lifetime away from everyone and everything I knew back home. It wasn't all bad, though. On my second-last night in Fairbanks, before making the journey back to Canada to tie up some loose ends, we hit the gold Alaska is really known for: the Northern Lights. It was a cold autumn night, but Alex (one of the camera guys I had become good friends with) and I, and some of the other crew, spent a couple of hours lying in a field near our accommodation, waiting for the lights to come out. It didn't take long before they showed in full force as dancing greens and blues throughout the sky: moving quick, dodging and changing direction, they put on a better light show than any attempt humans have made. As we lay there in awe, I jokingly said the only thing that could make the night better was if the wolves started howling—and, just like that, they did. It was uncanny. We lay there for half an hour, watching the lights swim through the sky and listening to the wolves howl louder than I had ever heard them. It was the best Alaskan experience I could have asked for to end a wild couple of months living there.

As I drove out of Fairbanks I felt a great sense of achievement. Even though we'd had some big losses, we also had some big wins. We had managed to get a mining operation off the ground with miners we had never met before they were hired, in a brand-new country, mining in ground we had no idea how to read, all with my help—me, a brand-new mine manager in a brand-new role! I also felt so blessed that this is my life: I was living my dream job and I was just so thankful for every opportunity that was coming my way. It was a pretty surreal feeling. I felt very lucky.

I didn't know what was in store for me next, but after my time in Alaska, I had proven to myself that I was a capable prospector, miner, and businesswoman in my own right. I had battled not only the elements but my own self-doubt and mental health issues, and came out on top. Of course, while I owe a lot of my success to my friends and family, I owe a lot of it to Tyler from ten years ago. I wish she could see who she's become: a confident, intelligent, successful woman with a future full of gold ahead of her.

ACKNOWLEDGMENTS

Thank you to my beautiful family—all of my successes are because of you. Mum, Dad, and Reece: thank you from the bottom of my heart for supporting every insane idea I have, and constantly being my safety net. You have always been my biggest cheer squad, my shoulders to cry on, and the first people I turn to when I need help. You have always believed in me, even when I didn't believe in myself. Sharon, Damien, Jaxon, Tatum, and Demi: thank you for being my second set of parents, and my additional brother and sisters. All of my best memories involve you, and I am so grateful for everything you have done for me.

Thank you to my absolute soulmates Sarah, Sophie, and Kyah, who have been right by my side through every high and every low, and have never made me feel like I am too much. One of my biggest achievements in life is calling you three my best friends, and I will never take for granted how lucky we are to share a bond so strong. Thank you also to all of my other friends who are in my corner, even when I spend months at a time on the other side of the world. All of you have been a part of my journey and nothing in this book would be possible without you.

Thank you so much to Jake's family and friends for being such a huge part of my world and welcoming me so warmly into their circles. Tina, Shane, Megan and Kobey, and Kaili and Lew—I feel so blessed to have you in my life.

A huge thank you to Affirm Press for giving me a chance to tell my story. I felt so at home with everyone involved from the very first Zoom call, and I am so grateful for that. Thank you to Martin and Armelle for always reminding me to just be myself; you gave me the confidence to keep going even when I felt like everything I wrote was horrible. To everyone else involved in the process—Bonnie, Rosie, Laura, and Susie—without you, this book would be nothing but a far-fetched dream! You have all helped me every step of the way to make this everything I hoped for.

To Shane, Ashleigh, and Ben at Stage Addiction: thank you so much for taking me under your wing and opening so many doors for me! This book wouldn't be possible without you all.

Lastly, to my beautiful partner, Jake—thank you endlessly for your undying support and love for me and my career. You have never once made me question myself or my career choices, and you selflessly put my job before us with no questions asked. I feel like I have known you for a lifetime, and I have never been around someone who makes me feel this much comfort, safety, and love. I wouldn't want to get matching tattoos twenty-four hours after meeting with anyone else! Thank you for everything, and I can't wait for a future with you.

MENTAL HEALTH RESOURCES

If you're in immediate danger or need urgent assistance, call 911.

If you'd like to get help with your mental health or an eating disorder, you can contact the following services.

The National Suicide Prevention Lifeline
Call or text 988; You can also use Lifeline Chat on the web (988lifeline.org). Both are available 24/7.

Substance Abuse and Mental Health Services Administration (SAMHSA)
A free resource for individuals who are looking for help or referrals to mental health providers. They can be reached 24/7 by calling 1-800-662-4357.

Crisis Text Line
Users can text the word "HOME" to 741741 to connect with a crisis counselor for free. This service is available 24/7.